CHILDREN AT RISK

DR. JAMES DOBSON
and Gary L. Bauer

CHILDREN AT RISK

The Battle for the Hearts and Minds of Our Kids

WORD PUBLISHING
Dallas · London · Vancouver · Melbourne

CHILDREN AT RISK

Copyright © 1990 by James C. Dobson and Gary L. Bauer

Unless otherwise indicated, Scripture quotations are from the New International Version of the Bible, published by the Zondervan Corpo-ration, copyright © 1973 by the New York Bible Society. Used by per-mission. Those marked KJV are from the King James Version.

Library of Congress Cataloging-in-Publication Data

Dobson, James C., 1936–
    Children at risk : the battle for the hearts and minds of our kids
  /   by James C. Dobson and Gary L. Bauer.
        p.   cm.
    Includes bibliographical references.
    ISBN 0-8499-0703-9
    1. Child rearing—Religious aspects—United States.   2. Children—United States—Religious life.   3. Family—United States.   4. Child welfare—United States.   5. United States—Moral conditions.
    I. Bauer, Gary Lee, 1946–   .   II. Title.
    HQ769.3.D62   1990
    649'.1—dc20   90-46932
                                                                                  CIP

Printed in the United States of America

0 1 2 3 4 9 AGM 9 8 7 6 5 4 3 2 1

This book is affectionately dedicated to families everywhere who are struggling to survive the pressures and threats of the late twentieth century. It has been our purpose to encourage them and plead their cause.

Specifically, we are dedicating our writings to the families we know and love best, in gratitude and love:

Shirley, Danae, and Ryan Dobson

Carol, Elyse, Sarah, and Zachary Bauer

CONTENTS

James C. Dobson

1

THE CHANGING WORLD OF CHILDREN

His name is Josh and he is three years old. He's the kind of kid you want to hug, with his cute blonde hair, infectious smile, and winsome personality. His father brings Josh to the gymnasium three mornings each week where he plays on the sidelines while his dad and a few aging jocks sweat it out on the basketball court. That's where I met him.

One day during a break in the action, I walked over to the bleachers and sat down beside Josh. I tried a couple of times to engage him in conversation, but got nowhere. He didn't really know me and he was perfectly willing to leave it that way. After getting no more than a nod in response to several questions, I resorted to the "can't miss, never fail" method of making friends with a small boy.

I said, "Josh, have you ever been stung by a bee?"

He lit up like a Christmas tree.

"Yeah," he said excitedly. "He got me right there," pointing to the side of his big toe.

"Did you step on him?" I asked.

"Nope. He dived on me," said Josh.

From that point on, Josh and I were fast friends. We kicked a volleyball back and forth and talked about things that turned him on. Nothing, however, interested him quite like the bee that "dived" from the sky and grabbed his big toe.

I smiled as I watched little Josh running around the gymnasium gleefully teasing his father and chasing loose basketballs. He reminded me of my own kids, now grown, and the joy they brought to our house during their preschool years.

Then a certain sadness came over me. I thought about the 25 million little babies who have been killed through abortion since the Supreme Court legalized their slaughter in 1973. Their numbers would amount to ten percent of today's entire population of Americans.

Each of those tiny infants had the potential to be like Josh—incredibly precious, worth more than the combined wealth of the entire world. If they had been permitted to live, six million of them would now be journeying through the teenage years and pressing toward adulthood. Nearly eleven million would be in elementary school, carrying their Crayolas and Mickey Mouse lunch boxes to class each morning.

Then I looked again at Josh. Incredibly, more than a million of those nameless, faceless aborted babies would now be three years old, like my little friend there in the gym. They would be toddling and giggling and hugging the necks of their parents today. I tried to imagine that sea of humanity—a million little bundles of energy—who were savagely dismembered and poisoned before they could even plead for their lives. Something within me screamed, "No, it can't be!" But alas, the killing continues to this hour.

Not only do I mourn for those millions of babies who were taken from their places of safety, but I also worry about Josh and his contemporaries who *were* permitted to live. Theirs will not be an easy journey, either. The same twisted philosophy that permits us to kill infants with impunity is now prevalent throughout the Western world.

This strange new way of thinking has produced a society that is incredibly dangerous to young minds and bodies. Compare, if you will, today's environment for kids with the world into which I was born. I attempted to describe my own adolescent experience in the following illustration from an earlier book about children.

> I attended high school during the "Happy Days" of the 1950s, and I never saw or even heard of anyone taking an illegal drug. It happened, I suppose, but it was certainly no threat to me. Some of the other students liked to get drunk, but alcohol was not a big deal in my social environment. Others played around with sex, but the girls who did were considered "loose" and were not respected. Virginity was still in style for males and females. Occasionally a girl came up pregnant, but she was packed off in a hurry and I never knew where she went. Homosexuals were very weird and unusual people. I heard there were a few around but I didn't know them personally. Most of my friends respected their parents, went to church on Sunday, studied hard enough to get by and lived a fairly clean life. There were exceptions, of course, but this was the norm. It's no wonder that my parents were concentrating on other anxieties.[1]

Perhaps I overstated the case. I'm sure those earlier years were not as tranquil or moral as I recall. Nevertheless, the cultural gap between that time and this is a million miles wide, and most of the changes occurring in the world of children have been for the worse.

This point was emphasized for me recently when I happened to watch a television documentary on the subject of elephants, of all things. No, it did not address the needs of children, but it spoke to me about the younger generation and the tragic mistakes we are making in their upbringing.

The program was videotaped in India, where magnificent pachyderms are trained to serve their human masters. Of course, if elephants knew how strong they were they would never yield to the domination of anything, but they are subjected to stressful forms of "brainwashing," which takes the fight out of them.

The process begins with three days of total isolation from man or beast. Female elephants and their young are remarkably social animals, and they react to loneliness the same way humans do. They grieve and fret and long for their peers. At that precise moment of vulnerability, they are brought to a nighttime ceremony of fire. Then, for many hours in the flickering light, they are screamed at, intimidated, stroked and ordered back and forth. By morning, half-crazed, the elephants have yielded. Their wills have been broken. Man is the master. Even though I understand the economic need for working elephants in India, there is still something sad about their plight. These wonderfully intelligent animals are transformed from freedom to slavery in a single evening. Their fragile emotions are manipulated to destroy their independence and curb their individuality. Somehow, I wish it weren't true.

Then as I watched the documentary, I was struck by the parallel between these elephants and us fragile human beings. We, too, are social creatures, born with irrepressible needs to be loved and accepted by our parents and peers. In fact, to deprive us of this emotional support during early childhood is to risk crippling us for life.

But if our needs for love are great during childhood, they can't compare with the soul hunger we feel with the arrival of adolescence. Like the elephants staked in a distant field, teenagers are subjected by their culture to a period of intense isolation and loneliness. Even those who are moderately successful during these years often feel rejected, ridiculed and ignored.

Unfortunately, for the most tender and pliable among us, the pain of adolescence can be incalculable. These youngsters slink through the halls of their schools, looking at the floor and fearing the wrath of their peers. They are, at that moment, prime targets for brainwashing. Adolescent society will do the rest.

Conditioning and Conformity

Anyone who has worked with teenagers has surely witnessed this mind-bending process at work. Television and movies hammer away at moral values and principles. Friends and acquaintances ridicule any form of self-discipline or restraint. But the analogy to the conditioning of elephants becomes even more striking.

Rock concerts subject masses of emotionally needy kids to deafening noises, eerie lights, wild behavior, and godless philosophies. Like an elephant during the night of fire, an adolescent begins to lose his grip on reality. His fight to preserve individuality slowly ebbs away. A passion for conformity rises from deep within. His peer group becomes lord and master, until finally, the wonderful freedom of youth is traded for slavery and domination.

This conditioning process helps explain the irrationality of youth. Why else would healthy boys and girls inject wretched drugs into their veins—or give sexual favors to a virtual stranger—or dye their hair orange and green—or even commit suicide? Their behavior has been warped by enormous social pressures in an environment of unmet needs.

Obviously, teenagers possess a free will and I would not excuse those who engage in irresponsible behavior. But they are also victims—victims of a peer-dominated society that often leaves them lost and confused. And my heart goes out to them.

How passionately I feel about the plight of today's children. How sorry I am for the pressures we have allowed to engulf them. How regretful I am for the sexual enticements that reach their ears during elementary school—teaching them that virginity is a curse and sex an adolescent toy. How I grieve for the boys and girls who have been told, and now they believe, that they are utter fools and will fail in each of life's endeavors.

How tender I feel toward the wounded children, the blind or deaf, or overweight, or retarded or cerebral palsied, who believe themselves to be cursed by God and man. Somehow, we must make a new effort to reach this generation with a message of confidence and hope and love and respect.

To build a bridge of hope to the young, we must get a better understanding of the world in which they live. Perhaps it will be helpful to think of today's teenager as being compelled symbolically to walk alone down a long, dark corridor leading toward adulthood. On either side of this gloomy hall are many large doors, each bearing identifying words at eye level. They are called *Alcohol, Marijuana, Hard Drugs, Pornography, Gambling, Homosexual Experimentation, Premarital Sex*, on and on.

Every form of addictive behavior is represented by at least one door which the teenager must pass on his journey to maturity. As he approaches each portal, he can hear boisterous laughter and gaiety from within. His friends— or people he *wants* as friends—are already inside, and they are obviously having a blast.

Every now and then he hears someone call his name and beckon him to the party. Who knows what unimaginable thrills and sensations and sense of belonging can be waiting behind one of the doors? And why shouldn't he experience what everyone else is doing? Who—tell me—

who has the right to keep him locked out there in the dark by himself? His parents? That's a laugh.

They had their day, now it's his turn. Brilliant light shines from under each door, and the shadows of dancing bodies cast an eerie reflection on his adolescent face. Pounding music throbs in his ears. That does it! Forget the consequences! He reaches for the doorknob.

Consequences of Experimentation

For a certain percentage of individuals who open one or more of these dangerous doors (the probability varies for each addictive behavior), a tragedy begins to unfold. The susceptible adolescent must simply crack the door an inch or two and a monster will run out and grab its wide-eyed victim. Some, but not all, will be held in its power for the rest of their lives.

My wife's father was an alcoholic for more than 35 years. His inability to control his drinking and the violence it caused eventually destroyed his home and wounded everyone he loved. He died a lonely and regretful man with very little to show for his 77 years on this earth. How did it happen?

Did he plan to waste his entire salary each week and terrorize his little family? Of course not. He promised a thousand times to quit drinking. But the monster grabbed him during his teen years, and soon became his lord and master. He cracked open a door that should have remained shut. This young man never dreamed he was one of the individuals most vulnerable to liquor, and it eventually destroyed everything of value to him.

It is common knowledge that hard drugs are often instantly addictive and can hold their victims in a state of stupor for decades—or until early death sets them free. How many teenagers do you know who cracked the door to cocaine ever so slightly, and then found themselves locked in the embrace of a tyrannical habit? It happens every day.

Fewer people realize how incredibly addictive pornography is to most boys during early adolescence. *One* exposure at just the right moment can capture a susceptible young man on the verge of manhood. He then begins a masturbatory habit that feeds on ever more explicit and violent material.

Like most addictions, pornography is *progressive* in nature. Photographs and erotic literature that stimulate sexual excitement quickly lose their power. The viewer wants more, more, more! Sooner or later, he comes to the end of the line—where he has seen everything a man and woman can do together. He has viewed the human body from every angle until it is no longer erotic to him. What then? Indeed, what then?

For a percentage of men (that precise number is unknown), they will progress past this natural barrier to an interest in perverse behaviors, or "paraphilias" as they are called. These men lust after the most wretched material on earth, including child molestation and simulated murder, homosexual violence and explicit sodomy, sex between women and bulls or stallions or boars, spreading feces or urine on the body, etc. One might wonder how in the world a person could be stimulated by such unthinkably evil depictions. The answer typically involves an early addiction to soft core pornography which progresses, *for some individuals,* to the worst possible conclusion.

Though the media still thinks he was lying, Ted Bundy told me of his journey from "detective story" type pornography to hard core material depicting extreme violence toward women. He remained at that point in the progressive process for nearly two years before killing his first coed. By the time he was executed in Florida State Prison, he had raped and murdered at least 28 women and girls.

Very few men take a pornographic addiction this far, of course, but Bundy was certainly not the only one. I hear from other men on death row who tell similar stories. In Bundy's case, it began with the accidental discovery of "girlie magazines" at a roadside dump. He was about 13 at the time . . . and the fatal door was breached.

It should be clear that our job as parents, pastors, and youth leaders must be to keep the hallway of doors locked and barred to the adolescent traveler. That is precisely what I experienced as a teenager. The doors were securely closed and most of my friends were out in the corridor with me. What concerns me today is that the doors are not only unlocked for many kids—they are standing wide open!

The Thorny Path

The pathway to premature sex is particularly accessible to every bright-eyed youngster looking for a thrill. Brass bands, confetti, party favors, and condoms are distributed to the curious at the entrance—by adults who should know better. It's no wonder that the kids who want to remain chaste often feel like prudes and freaks today.

Pornographic music videos, raunchy television and teen sexploitation movies, such as *Porkeys* and *Fast Times at Ridgemont High*, make it clear that everybody's doing it. Whatever natural barriers and modesty that might have existed between the sexes is quickly circumvented.

In that kind of world, it should not surprise us that kids are participating in every form of sexual experimentation at a younger and younger age. This is especially true of females. The National Center for Health Statistics reports that 29 percent of 15 year-old girls are sexually active, and 81 percent of 19 year-olds! Boys are no less active. Seventy-two percent of 17 year-old boys are sexually active as well as 88 percent of 19 year-olds.

The consequence of this promiscuity is appalling. Not only are 1.5 million abortions occurring each year, but the spread of some 38 sexually transmitted diseases continues at epidemic proportions. For example, there were 27,000 cases of syphilis reported in 1986—a dangerous trend that captured national attention. But by 1989, the figure had risen to 44,000—an increase of 62 percent in just three years! A strain of gonorrhea has now appeared that is completely resistant to all known antibiotics.

Twenty to thirty percent of college-aged women are currently estimated to have genital herpes—a disease from which they will suffer the rest of their lives. And another virus known as HPV causes genital warts and cervical cancer in some infected women. The disease is untreatable and would be grabbing headlines if it weren't for the more serious AIDS epidemic.

Numerous other problems result from unbridled promiscuity, of course, including infertility and even death. And who can minimize the effects of sexual experimentation on subsequent marital relationships? Clearly, the door marked "Premarital Sex" is a passage to pain for those who would stroll through its portals.

Given the heartache and illness wreaked by adolescent promiscuity, one would expect responsible adults to be united in their opposition to it. Unfortunately, that is simply not the case. In fact, an aggressive campaign is under way to guarantee that young men and women continue to do what comes naturally.

I met a few of these campaigners face-to-face when I served on the Teen Pregnancy Prevention Panel for the Department of Health and Human Services. I assumed when I accepted the appointment from Secretary Otis Bowen that our purpose was to design programs to help curb adolescent promiscuity. That is generally thought to be the best way to prevent unplanned pregnancies. I was wrong.

My fellow panelists had a better idea. I made the mistake during our first session of mentioning the word "abstinence" to them and they reacted with alarm. First, they blanched, then began sweating, trembling and gasping for air. Obviously, I had struck a raw nerve.

I learned later that 15 of the 18 panel members wanted to teach the kids how to have lots of really fun safe-sex without making babies. That was their hidden agenda. When my two colleagues (Dr. Bill Pierce and Dr. Terrance Olson) and I realized that the deck had been stacked and that our panel would soon issue recommendations to distribute condoms and immoral advice to students attending the nation's schools, we resigned publicly at a Washington, D.C. press conference. But the tide rolled on and the effort to encourage adolescent sexuality soon became evident throughout our entire culture.

Legislating Immorality

Let's deal with the obvious question head on: Why do bureaucrats and researchers and Planned Parenthood types fight so hard to preserve adolescent promiscuity? Why do they balk at the thought of intercourse occurring only in the context of marriage? Why have they completely *removed* the door marked "Premarital Sex" for a generation of vulnerable teenagers?

Their motivation is not that difficult to understand. Multiplied millions of dollars are generated each year in direct response to teenage sexual irresponsibility. Kids jumping into bed with each other is supporting entire industries of grateful adults. The abortion business alone brings in an estimated $600 million annually. Do you really believe the physicians, nurses, medical suppliers and bureaucrats who owe their livelihood to the killing of unborn babies would prefer that adolescents abstain until marriage?!

How about condom manufacturers or the producers of spermicide, "the pill," IUDs, or diaphragms? Would they want their business decimated by a sweeping wave or morality among the young? I doubt it. Then there are the producers of antibiotics and other drugs for use in treating sexually transmitted diseases. They have a financial stake in continued promiscuity, as well.

At the top of the list of those who profit from adolescent irresponsibility, however, are those who are purportedly working to fight it! Planned Parenthood and similar organizations would simply fade away if they were ever fully successful in eliminating teen pregnancies. They currently receive an estimated $106 million in federal subsidies to carry out their mission, plus approximately $200 million in contributions from private sources. Do you *really* believe they want to kill the goose that lays those golden eggs?

Imagine how many jobs would be lost if kids quit playing musical beds with one another! This is why professionals who advise young people about sex are so emotional about the word *abstinence*. If that idea ever caught on, who would need the services of Planned Parenthood and their ilk? It's a matter of self-preservation.

To fully comprehend the danger posed by Planned Parenthood and related organizations, it is important to examine their philosophy and intent. What is their program? What do their leaders want? What would they do if given free rein? As I understand their agenda, it can be summarized in the following four-point plan:

1. **Provide "value-free" guidance on sexuality to teenagers.** Heaven forbid any preference for morality or sexual responsibility being expressed.
2. **Provide unlimited quantities of contraceptives to adolescents**, dispensed aggressively from clinics located on junior and senior high campuses. In

so doing, a powerful statement is made to teen-agers about adult approval of premarital sexual activity.

3. **Keep parents out of the picture by every means possible.** Staff members for Planned Parenthood can then assume the parental role and communicate their libertarian philosophy to teens.

4. **Provide unlimited access to free abortions for young women who become pregnant**; again, without parental involvement or permission.

Incredibly, the American and Canadian public seems to "buy" this outrageous plan, which would have brought a storm of protest from yesterday's parents. Imagine how your father or grandfather would have reacted if a school official had secretly given contraceptives to you or arranged a quiet abortion when you were a teenager. The entire community would have been incensed.

Someone may well have been shot! Yet today's parents have tolerated this intrusion without so much as a peep of protest. Why? What has happened to that spirit of protection for our families—that fierce independence that bonded us together against the outside world? I wish I knew.

No Safe Sex

Many people apparently believe that Planned Parenthood's approach will reduce the incidence of adolescent pregnancy. Not only is that illogical, but research is demonstrating the folly of helping teenagers experience so-called "safe sex."

As Planned Parenthood has grown in income and influence, the rates of unwed pregnancy and abortion among teens have skyrocketed. Furthermore, a comprehensive study conducted by Stan Weed and Joseph Olsen at the Institute for Research and Evaluation reveals that the Planned

Parenthood approach actually *worsens* rather than resolves the problem of adolescent sexuality.

Weed and Olsen compared rates of pregnancy, abortion and live births on a state-by-state basis. They concluded that, all things being equal, for every 1,000 teens between 15 and 19 years of age enrolled in family planning clinics, we can expect between 50 to 100 more pregnancies! Their study, based on Planned Parenthood's own data, also revealed significant contradictions between the organization-projected *decreases* in pregnancy and abortion rates, compared with actual increases in both categories. The researchers concluded, "When a program clearly should work, but apparently doesn't, it is important to find out why." The reason is painfully obvious!

Admittedly, a serious problem does exist with regard to unwed adolescent pregnancy. "Children having children" is a tragedy which must be addressed in North America, and we have no time to lose. What, then, is the best way to approach the matter? What counterproposal do we offer to parents and educators? As with the approach by Planned Parenthood, our concept can also be summarized by a four-part plan:

1. Secure the involvement of parents in the system. Even though there are exceptions to the rule, no one has greater influence on teenagers that the mothers and fathers who have raised them. We *must not* permit the state or its self-appointed "saviors" to undermine parents and weaken their authority.

Parents hold the keys to responsible behavior. *In every state where parental consent for abortion has been reinstated, the incidences of teen pregnancy, abortion, and births have dropped dramatically.* After parental consent was mandated in Minnesota between 1980–83, births declined 23 percent for 12–17 year-olds, abortions decreased 40 percent and pregnancies fell 32 percent. In Rhode Island (1981–83), births declined 2 percent for

12–17 year-olds, abortion decreased 44 percent and pregnancies fell 30 percent. In Massachusetts (1980–82), pregnancies decreased 15 percent for 12–17 year-olds. The facts speak for themselves.

2. Teach sexual abstinence to teenagers, just as we attempt to teach them to abstain from drug and alcohol usage and other harmful behavior. Of course we can do it! Young people are fully capable of understanding that irresponsible sex is not in their best interest—that it leads to disease, unwanted pregnancy, rejection, and disappointment.

In many cases today, *no one* is sharing this truth with teenagers. Parents are embarrassed to talk about sex, and—it hurts me to say it—churches are often unwilling to address the issue. That creates a vacuum into which liberal sex counselors have intruded to say, "We know you're going to have sex anyway. Here's how to do it right!"

What an unfortunate message that is. Little support is provided even for the young person who is desperately looking for a valid reason to say "no." We have convinced him that "safe sex" is available if he'll just use the right equipment. He must be taught that there is no safety—*no place to hide*—when one lives in contradiction to the moral laws of God!

3. Remove the incentives for teens to become pregnant. Today an adolescent girl can obtain her own apartment and several hundred dollars per month from the government for having a baby out of wedlock. Why should it surprise us that a large number of frustrated, rebellious females, angry at their parents and anxious to escape parental authority, are deliberately allowing themselves to become pregnant?

The government has provided all the incentives necessary to establish countless welfare dependencies that may continue for generations. Instead, Aid to Families with Dependent Children (AFDC) should be provided to unmarried teenage mothers *only* if they remain home with their parents.

4. Finally, we should lead our children into an early and deeply meaningful relationship with Jesus Christ. The motivation and strength to live a life of purity is a by-product of this spiritual commitment and understanding.

Obviously, this Christian emphasis cannot be made in public schools. We can, however, teach the basics of the Judeo-Christian value system which has permeated our society for hundreds of years.

Included in this instruction should be the nature of the family, how it was designed to function, and why sexual exclusivity is such an essential component of marital happiness. Yes! It can be taught. Yes! It *must* be taught! No! Planned Parenthood will not teach it to our children.

To be entirely fair, we must acknowledge that Planned Parenthood and the other advocates of "safe sex" philosophies are not the only ones who want our children to open dangerous doors. My wife and I recently stayed in a hotel where hundreds of student leaders had been brought together, all expenses paid, by a major brewery. One need not guess why. Beer companies routinely give kegs of their best brew to fraternity and sorority houses, obviously hoping to entice young men and women to greater alcohol consumption.

Tobacco manufacturers also pitch their ads to the young because they know non-smoking older folks are not going to touch the stuff. Over one million kids adopt the habit every year, keeping cigarette companies in business.

Finally, the sellers of pornography in rock music and the producers of immoral television and movies have your children in mind. In short, there can be little doubt that the hallway of doors was erected largely by profit-minded adults who want the patronage of today's teenagers and the money that burns in their pockets.

Accepting the Challenge

What should we do, then, to get our sons and daughters safely down the long, dark corridor and on to the relative stability of adulthood? We have seen that we cannot yield control of those who would profit from youthful passion and irresponsibility. Nor can we abdicate our leadership to teachers, coaches, physicians, or others who do not share our moral and ethical values.

Our job as parents is to lock and bolt the doors that lead to addictive and harmful behavior. Stand guard in the hallway! Intercept the destructive messages being given to our vulnerable kids. Distract them with better alternatives when the temptations are greatest. Stay tuned in! Get involved! Fight for what you believe! And never forget that the children of over committed, harassed, exhausted parents are sitting ducks for the con men of our time!

In case you haven't noticed, this book is about children, yours and mine, and the environment in which they are being raised and educated. It is also about our grandkids and the many generations to come. They are the true wealth of any nation and in them lies the hope of the future. Without them, there *is* no future—no freshness, no springtime, no youthful vigor.

Indeed, a society that is too busy and too preoccupied for its children is just a nation of aging, dying people who feed on their own selfish interests.

If we agree on that basic premise, then we should take a cold, hard look at what we are doing to the most precious and vulnerable members of our society. We shall continue that critical examination in the chapters that follow. For now, let me give a final message to my young friend in the gymnasium. With the help of God, little Josh, we *will* build a safer, saner, more moral world in which you and your generation can grow. It is our profound duty, and we *will* meet it!

James C. Dobson

2

THE SECOND GREAT CIVIL WAR

In the previous chapter, I attempted to describe the effort to manipulate this generation of kids and the financial factors that motivate it. Now let me put that struggle in its larger context.

Something far more significant than money is behind the contest for the hearts and minds of children. Nothing short of a great Civil War of Values rages today throughout North America. Two sides with vastly differing and incompatible worldviews are locked in a bitter conflict that permeates every level of society.

Bloody battles are being fought on a thousand fronts, both inside and outside of government. Open any daily newspaper and you'll find accounts of the latest Gettysburg, Waterloo, Normandy, or Stalingrad.

Instead of fighting for territory or military conquest, however, the struggle now is for the hearts and minds of the people. It is a war over *ideas*. And someday soon, I believe, a winner will emerge and the loser will fade from memory. For now, the outcome is very much in doubt.

On one side of this Continental Divide are the traditionalists whose values begin with the basic assumption that "God *is . . .*" From that understanding comes a far reaching system of thought that touches every dimension of life. Their beliefs are deeply rooted in Scripture, beginning with the Ten Commandments and continuing through New Testament teachings and the gospel of Jesus Christ.

Adherents believe (1) in lifelong marriage; (2) in the value of bearing and raising children; (3) in the traditional family, meaning individuals related by marriage, birth or adoption; (4) in the universal worth of the individual, regardless of productivity or other contributions to mankind; and (5) in a complex series of immutable truths, including premarital chastity, fidelity and loyalty between spouses, the value of self-discipline and hard work, and more.

On virtually every moral issue of the day, the conservative, Christian perspective can be found in scriptural understandings. For example, consider the practices of abortion, infanticide and euthanasia. Attitudes toward these forms of murder are shaped by words that were spoken 4,000 years ago, including this passage: "This day I call heaven and earth as witnesses against you that I have set before you life and death, blessings and curses. Now choose life, so that you and your children may live" (Deuteronomy 30:19 NIV). Countless other illustrations could be cited.

Until approximately thirty years ago, these biblically based concepts were the dominant values and beliefs in Western society. Not everyone agreed, of course, but most did. Decisions made in Congress or by the judicial system typically reflected this broad understanding. And you can be sure that the public schools also conformed to it. Parents saw to that.

Then, slowly at first, another way of looking at the world began to emerge. It evolved from the basic assumption that "God isn't . . ." Everything emanating from the Creator was jettisoned, including reverence for Scripture or any of the transcendent, universal truths. "Right" was determined by what *seemed* right at a particular time.

All the old rules and commandments had to be reconsidered. Since in their view human beings have no eternal significance, the value of life was cheapened. Our species became just another member of the animal kingdom, perhaps brighter than the rest, but of no more value. Thus, secular humanists easily embraced abortion, infanticide, and euthanasia when convenience demanded.

Historic perspectives on morality and ethics gave way to a "new morality" based on changing social attitudes. Prohibitions dissolved, rules changed, restrictions faded, and guilt subsided. Obviously, this moral free-fall was very liberating in the early days, as self-discipline and restraint yielded to a less demanding master. And it caught on like wildfire.

A Wasteland of Values

It has been said that never in human history has a culture discarded its belief system more quickly than America did in the sixties, or so it seemed at the time. I remember hearing a television producer say in 1967 that within ten years we could expect to see unedited depictions of sexual intercourse in a movie made for the general public. His statement shocked me and I expressed disbelief to my wife.

I thought it would never happen. As it turned out, the producer was only partially correct. It happened *one* year later when the movie *I Am Curious Yellow* was released in the U.S., featuring a nude man and woman engaged in simulated sexual intercourse on the silver screen. It was followed by *Deep Throat* and other obscene productions that enjoyed surprisingly popular appeal. The sexual revolution was on.

The humanistic system of values has now become the predominant way of thinking in most of the power centers of society. It has outstripped Judeo-Christian precepts in the universities, in the news media, in the entertainment industry, in the judiciary, in the federal bureaucracy, in business, medicine, law, psychology, sociology, in the arts, in many public schools and, to be sure, in the halls of Congress. Indeed, the resources available to secular humanists throughout society are almost unlimited in scope, and they are breaking new ground almost every day.

Where, then, are the strongholds of the Judeo-Christian ethic? Only two bulwarks remain, and they both face unrelenting pressure from the left. The first is the Christian church, which has been on the defensive in recent years and has lost its taste for battle.

There are many exceptions, of course, and some of the most effective work done in the pro-life or anti-pornography movements is emanating from the institution of the church. By and large, however, *individuals* have carried the banner while many denominational leaders have been reluctant to get involved. Some pastors and congregations feel severely wounded by the highly publicized scandals in the "televised church" toward the end of the eighties.

Thus, the churches have pulled within their own fortresses to avoid becoming "political," and therefore, vulnerable to ridicule. Meanwhile, 25 million babies have died, obscenity abounds everywhere, our values and symbols are mocked incessantly on television, our children are corrupted by movies and MTV, and our Congressional leaders are steadily encroaching upon our constitutional freedoms.

While all of this is going on, many of us in the church

go about our business and pretend not to notice. The great army of believers could still turn the tide of battle if it awakens in time, but thus far only a courageous minority has been willing to defend the beloved homeland with their lives.

The second repository of Judeo-Christian values is the institution of the family. Alas, the beleaguered, exhausted, oppressed, and overtaxed family now stands unprotected against a mighty foe. If it collapses, and if the church fails to mobilize, the Civil War will be over in a matter of days.

From this perspective, it should be clear why these two institutions are under such vicious attack from so many quarters today. They alone stand in opposition to vast cultural changes, planned and promoted by the social engineers.

I will not take the time here to list or describe the specific attempts by secular humanists to weaken the institution of the family and the church, but they are legion. A single example will suffice. On May 4–5, 1989, the American Bar Association conducted a seminar in the city of San Francisco. It was devoted entirely to suggested methods of litigating against religious institutions.

Workshops were offered on such subjects as "Expanding Use of Tort Law Against Religions," "Liability of Clergy as Spiritual Counselors," and "Liability of Religious Bodies and Affiliated Entities." The workshop that best illustrates ABA's motives, however, was the one titled, "Tort Law as an Ideological Weapon."

Note that the stated purpose of such indoctrination was not merely to help clients gain recompense for wrongs done by the church. It was to use litigation as an "ideological weapon" against religious institutions. The avowed target of the ABA, representing 335,807 attorneys and vast financial resources, is the very soul of the Christian church.

The Changing World Order

What will life be like in the Western world if secular humanists prevail in the struggle for social dominance? What kind of revisions will be made in our moral code, in our civil laws, and in our daily lives if the restraining influence of traditional and scriptural wisdom is abandoned? Especially, how will the institution of the family be changed if society slides away from the Judeo-Christian heritage?

To my knowledge, those questions have never been answered by those who would take us into a brave new world. Still, we can draw inferences from court decisions, medical experiments, and governmental policies that emanate from the humanistic agenda.

We were given a glimpse of left-wing-logic when a California court ruled in the case of *Curlender v. Bio-Science Laboratories*, 1980,*, 1 that a mother *must* have an abortion if medical science indicates that her child will be born with a serious birth defect. Failure to do so will allow the child to sue his parents for damages in later years! Believe it or not, that is what the judge ruled.

From this and other developments in the movement, we can predict that "forced abortion" to control family size would be imposed upon us. That has already occurred in China, of course. The Chinese policy of permitting only one child per couple is applauded by NOW President, Molly Yard. She seems not the least disturbed that forced abortion has led to the deaths of millions of first-born babies who were unfortunate enough to be female. The consequence? According to a recent report filed by the Reuters News Service, there are now 689 single men for every 100 single women in China.[2]

---

* The California legislature subsequently adopted the Civil Code Section 43.6 in 1981 to prevent handicapped children from suing their parents for permitting birth to occur, although similar "wrongful life" rulings have been handed down in other courts.

As long as we are on the subject of crazy ideas, consider this article published in the American Bar Association's prestigious journal, *Family Law Quarterly*, in 1988. Written with guidance of the associate dean and professor of law at Georgetown University Law Center, it calls for the *licensing* of parents by the state. Unlicensed mothers and fathers would be required to give up their children for adoption. The author admitted that the system could be used against parents whose ideas of child rearing and family life are not in line with "community standards." Guess who they have in mind.[3]

How about the 1985 ruling by the Internal Revenue Service which declared that if a child is intentionally aborted but somehow manages to survive for two or more days before dying, he can be declared a dependent by the parents who attempted to kill him. That is pure secular humanism in action. Follow the logic now. The unborn child is aborted at his parents' request, but they are not charged with assault because he isn't deemed to be human in the eyes of the law.

But if he lives at least two days, he becomes a dependent for tax purposes because he *is* a child. But if he then dies a few hours later, his killers will not be charged with murder because he *isn't* a child. This is where the convoluted thinking of man leads us. We quickly cease to make sense when we abandon the wisdom of the Creator and substitute our own puny ideas of the moment.

Let's look more specifically at the definition of marriage and family life. How might it change if radical humanists were in charge? In this instance, the answer has been put forward. On the next page is a reproduction of an actual letter sent by the ACLU to the California State Assembly Education Committee. It was written in response to legislation which subsequently passed, mandating the teaching of abstinence in all California sex education programs.

ACLU

AMERICAN CIVIL LIBERTIES UNION
CALIFORNIA LEGISLATIVE OFFICE
1127 11th Street, Suite 605 □
Sacramento, California 95814
Telephone (916) 442-1036 □

May 26, 1988

Members, Assembly Education Committee
State Capitol
Sacramento, CA 95814

Re: SB 2394 - Oppose

Dear Members:

The ACLU regrets to inform you of our opposition to SB 2394
concerning sex education in public schools.

It is our position that teaching that monogamous, heterosexual intercourse within marriage is a traditional American
value is an unconstitutional establishment of a religious
doctrine in public schools. There are various religions which
hold contrary beliefs with respect to marriage and monogamy. We
believe SB 2394 violates the First Amendment.

If you or your staff wish to discuss this matter further, please
contact our office.

Very truly yours,

MARJORIE C. SWARTZ
Legislative Director

FRANCISCO LOBACO
Legislative Advocate

FL/rmc
cc: Consultant, Assembly Education Committee
    The Hon. Newton Russell, State Capitol, Room 5061, SAC 95814
    (Disc #2 Mis. Com. Ltrs. 88')

Marjorie C. Swartz, Legislative Director • Francisco Lobaco, Legislative Advocate • Rita M. Egri, Legislative Assistant
ACLU of Northern California • Dorothy M. Ehrlich, Executive Director ACLU of Southern California • Ramona Ripston, Executive Director
1663 Mission Street, Suite 460 • San Francisco, 94103 • (415)621-2493 633 South Shatto Place • Los Angeles, 90005 • (213) 487-1720

The institution of marriage has been a sacred bond of fidelity between a man and a woman in every civilization, in every culture, throughout recorded history. The pledge of loyalty and mutual support represented by the marriage vows is a promise of commitment which extends to every aspect of life—particularly to the sexual relationship between a husband and wife, forsaking all others. That is a time-honored truth.

This letter shows that it is the ACLU's position that "monogamous, heterosexual intercourse within marriage [as] a traditional value is an unconstitutional establishment of a religious doctrine . . . ." Expressed another way, anything that emanates from the Christian heritage is unconstitutional, and therefore, illegal. That is how the ACLU views the institution of marriage and the sexual fidelity upon which it is based.

Indeed, the ACLU, which spends upwards of 25 million dollars each year to advance its extremist views in the courts, is itself a major threat to the institution of the family. Consider, for example, its unbelievable perspective on child pornography. Their representative, Mr. Barry Lynn, testified in 1985 before the Attorney General's Commission on Pornography, on which I served as a member.

Mr. Lynn sat with a straight face and told us it was the ACLU's position that the sale and distribution of child pornography, once it is in existence, should not be prohibited by law. Anyone who gains access to such materials should be free to market them at will.

The implications of this incredible statement of policy are breathtaking. It means that the terrible molestation of a child, if photographed or videotaped during the crime, could be sold on newsstands for the profit of pornographers, and there would be nothing the child or his family could do to prevent the exploitation of this tragedy. The child would see his nude image in magazines or video tapes through the years, photographed during the most devastating experience of his life.

This is what the ACLU calls *civil liberties! Whose* civil liberties, we must ask? God help us if this organization and others which share its perverted philosophy ever gains the influence and control they seek!

Finally, I should mention one more monument to the humanist movement that came straight out of hell. A father dying of kidney failure artificially inseminated his 16 year-old daughter with the help of her physician. Seven months into her pregnancy, the child was taken from her uterus by cesarean section. Its kidneys were removed surgically and transplanted into the father (grandfather). The infant was then left to die of uremic poisoning.

If this sounds like something more likely to have occurred in Nazi Germany, it will be helpful to remember that the Nazis also made up their rules as they went along. And why not? What seems right *is* right, we are told.

These are not isolated "horror" stories drawn from the exceptional or unique. They are prime examples of humanistic thinking which help us understand the liberal mindset and identify its objectives. There is little doubt about where it hopes to take us! Furthermore, we get an even clearer picture of leftist thinking by examining the federal bureaucracies in operation. They have been guided by humanistic principles for at least three decades, and the consequence has been catastrophic.

The Liberal Power Block

The innumerable federal initiatives intended to assist children and families provide a prime example of warped liberal thinking. Billions of dollars have been spent by Congress on a dazzling array of programs to help the needy and disadvantaged.

Massive governmental structures have mushroomed in Washington in support of youth employment, food stamps, early childhood intervention, juvenile justice, delinquency prevention, social research, parental training, drug education, and other issues.

Hundreds of thousands of federal employees go to work each morning in agencies whose sole purpose is the welfare and betterment of children. Just one department of this bureaucracy, Health and Human Services, spends more than a billion dollars every day on countless social and welfare programs.

After decades of wild expenditures of this nature, it is appropriate that we ask what have we accomplished with these precious resources. What did we get for our money? Did the experts and the reformers deliver on their promises? Are our children better off now than before these programs began?

By almost any standard of measurement, the grand initiatives designed to assist children and families have been national disasters. Chaos reigns supreme in the inner cities where most of the effort was directed. The Black family in America has been virtually destroyed. Drug abuse is at an all time high. Alcoholism plagues young and old alike.

Suicide is currently a leading cause of death among the young. Teenagers are killing one another in gang warfare. The emergency wards of inner city hospitals can no longer handle the numbers of wounded and dying patients coming in for treatment. Twenty-five percent of all Black males are in jail or on probation or parole. Many young Black women are left with little hope of finding committed husbands with whom to build families.

Homeless people litter the street, sleeping on heating grates and digging for food in garbage cans. Sexual molestation of children is rampant. Physical abuse of kids is an everyday affair. Sexually transmitted diseases travel freely within the human family, and the HIV virus stalks the community of homosexuals. *This* is the legacy of secular humanism in the hands of big government.

And what about the crises in our schools? The National Education Association told us twenty years ago that their overriding problem was a lack of money. Student-teacher ratios were too high, they said. Equipment was old and outmoded.

Congress believed them, as Congress is wont to do. But now, after annual expenditures for elementary and secondary education have risen from 21.3 billion dollars in 1963 to 213 billion dollars in 1990, our schools are in worse shape than ever.

Student scores on the Scholastic Aptitude Test (SAT) have been on a slippery slope since 1960, and are still descending. Only 57 percent of the class of 1988 graduated from high school in Boston. In Washington, D.C. the figure is 58 percent; in Detroit it is 62 percent.

Test scores show that we are rapidly becoming a nation of illiterates, with a greater number of non-readers than almost any other industrialized nation. But, once again, the NEA is saying "more money is needed to do the job."

So where are the experts who promised us utopia a few years ago? Where is the vast army of psychologists, sociologists, physicians, academicians, theoreticians and ideologists who led us into the abyss? Why haven't they been held accountable for the mess they precipitated? Why hasn't Congress been called to explain their wastefulness to the American people? I can't answer those questions.

The Assault of Secularism

I *do* know that our erstwhile advisors are still out there today, busily designing *new* programs that will exhaust our resources and create the problems of tomorrow. As for Congress, it is happily squandering the wealth of this great nation. They are stealing from the next generation by unprecedented deficit spending. It is indeed a shame that future citizens could not be here to see how we are wasting *their* assets on such folly! It's enough to make a strong man weep.

Let me reemphasize my point, in case it has been missed. The problem with federal bureaucracies is not that their plans are poorly designed and implemented. It is that the philosophy which governs them is out of harmony with the immutable laws of the universe! It *can't* succeed because it is based on false and dangerous assumptions.

Social disruption is *inevitable* when government accepts these humanistic tenets: (1) committed, lifelong, faithful families are outmoded or expendable; (2) sexual experimentation of the young is healthy if done "right;" (3) education should be utterly valueless and relativistic; (4) there is no absolute right or wrong . . . no ultimate truth on which to base our decisions; (5) homosexual "preference" is simply another valid lifestyle; (6) he who *can* work but chooses idleness shall be sheltered and fed; (7) there is no God, and therefore, no transcendent purpose and meaning in living.

It is the application of these and other misguided concepts that has created social chaos in Western society today. And there is no end in sight.

As we have indicated, the humanist movement is far from embarrassed or discouraged about its failures. They accept no responsibility for our ills. Instead, activists are accelerating their drive for final victory and dominance. The following article in the *San Francisco Chronicle*, illustrates just one spearhead in this campaign:

A DRIVE TO RAISE GAY ISSUES IN STATE SCHOOL TEXTBOOKS

Gay and lesbian leaders have begun a campaign to have topics of concern to homosexuals included in textbooks used in California schools.

"We want to see that the contributions and triumphs of gay and lesbian people are talked about as openly as any other segments of the population," said Rob Birle, 33, a teacher in Antioch and a member of Bay Area Network of Gay and Lesbian Educators.

Birle said gay leaders want textbooks to include information on the sexual orientation of famous people in history and on the modern gay movement.[4]

Birle concluded his comments by saying, "We're gearing up for a long-term battle." I wonder if traditionalists are also gearing up for battle. I wonder if a sizable number of ordinary moms and dads *care* enough to oppose this proposition. If not, their sons and daughters will soon be sitting in fourth or sixth or eighth grade social studies classes, reading about the wonderful exploits of their homosexual and lesbian forefathers.

Unfortunately, so many people who share traditionalist views appear not to know a war is going on—a conflict that will have profound implications for future generations. By contrast, our opponents are highly motivated, well-funded, deeply committed and armed to the teeth. This fact becomes inescapable when one examines how issues of importance to the family are decided in governmental circles.

The Political Machinery

When hearings are being held in Congress on issues of significance to the family, you can be sure the American Civil Liberties Union will be there. The National Organization of Women will be there. Gay rights activists will be there. The National Abortion Rights Action League will be there. And Norman Lear's People for the American Way will be there. But where are *our* troops? Well, they're taking care of business back home in Indiana or Texas or Pennsylvania. Chances are they won't even know the issues are being discussed unless some lonely crier spreads the word. Even if information has been disseminated, conservative activists typically come in late and leave early. They have more important things to do.

In the absence of proper vigilance, therefore, the institution of the family is sustaining losses that threaten its very existence. Let me ask you where you were in the mid '70s when the national debate on parental consent for abortion was held? Did you participate in it? Did you know it was on going? Did you come to Washington to defend your point of view? Frankly, I didn't, because I was like millions of people—like you. I was preoccupied at home and thought someone else would look out for my interests in national policy. They didn't!

Without this representation, our rights are being stripped from us. For example, parents have held absolute authority for the medical care of their children for the past 200 years. It is illegal to disinfect a scratch or give an aspirin to another parent's son or daughter without their permission, and those who do so can be charged with battery. At times, that policy can be frightening.

Our son, Ryan, is a hotdog skier who loves to risk life and limb on mountain slopes. When he was 13 years old, he was burning through the trees on a snowy trail when he suddenly came over the top of a little hill. The hill turned out to be a seven foot cliff. Ryan fell from the sky and landed on his back. He was immediately knocked unconscious. When the ski patrol found him, a few minutes later, they put our son on a litter and transported him down the mountain to a first aid station.

At that point, even though they suspected that his back was broken or severely damaged, the medics were unable to examine him further. He lay on a gurney in the aid station for more than two hours while the ski patrol searched for Shirley and me. Why? Because the authority to provide medical care for Ryan rested entirely in our hands. That has been the law in Western society since colonial times.

How did it happen, then, that parents lost the right to know when their daughters were subjected to abortions? How was that decision made? Who represented the interests of parents when it was determined that a 13 or 14 year-old girl—who is still a child in many ways—could legally be *transported* by school officials to an abortionist, where a serious surgical procedure is performed without parental knowledge?

Her mother and father not only can't stop the abortion from occurring; they don't even have the right to be informed of it in *retrospect*. The child comes home that afternoon having been through an experience she will remember for the rest of her life, yet the parents who brought her into the world and nurtured her through childhood have been eliminated from the equation.

Furthermore, they are unaware of her precarious health. She could continue to bleed in the days ahead; she could get an infection; she could suffer emotional problems from consequent guilt or regret. No matter. Unless she chooses to tell her parents of the event, they will never know about it!

Suppose this young girl's family is profoundly committed to the pro-life position and believes passionately that abortion is murder. Maybe this conviction is a deeply held tenet of their faith. That's just too bad. Somewhere in the vast bureaucracies of government, a decision was made that deprived them of an ancient right, and then a dozen or more liberal judges issued rulings that set the policy in concrete.

That was all it took. And I assure you that newspaper and television commentators made no announcement to the public that the traditional family had just suffered another enormous defeat. Dan Rather said nothing. Tom Brokaw was silent. CNN ignored the story. It was a quiet victory for the humanists, like so many others occurring each day in the halls of government.

Suffering Silent Defeat

I think about these silent defeats every time I hear ministers admonish their congregations to avoid public debates, to leave governmental decisions exclusively in the hands of our elected officials, and to avoid unpleasant subjects in the church. They almost imply it is immoral for Christians to participate in this great representative form of government.

If Christians continue to do as these advisers suggest, we will yield the decision-making process entirely to the other side by default. We have as much right to influence the system as our philosophical opponents, and we *must* use the avenues guaranteed to us by the Constitution. Even as I write, other one-sided "debates" are in progress in the public arena that will continue to undermine the Judeo-Christian system of thought. It is an everyday affair.

Some will scoff at the suggestion that there is a coordinated, well thought out strategy to win this Civil War of Values. They might suggest that we are merely witnessing a casual and random drift of social mores, shifting over time from one end of the political spectrum to the other. I wish this were true, but it is not.

Secular humanists, particularly the more radical activists, have a specific objective in mind for the future. They hope to accomplish that goal primarily by isolating children from their parents, as they did so effectively with the parental consent issue. It will then be relatively easy to "reorient" and indoctrinate the next generation of Americans. This strategy explains why their most bitter campaigns are being waged over school curricula and other issues that involve our kids. Children are *the* key to the future.

Let me put it another way. Children are the prize to the winners of the second great civil war. Those who control what young people are taught and what they experience— what they see, hear, think, and believe—will determine the future course for the nation. Given that influence, the predominant value system of an entire culture can be overhauled in one generation, or certainly in two, by those with unlimited access to children.

There are several recent precedents that illustrate the effectiveness of the strategy I have described. Remember that Great Britain was deeply religious through the 1940s. Its culture was greatly influenced by Christian thought and values. Perhaps 60 to 70 percent of its population went to church each week, and the people and their leaders openly thanked God for sustaining them through the terrible war years. But that was then.

Today, only *three* percent of Britons consider themselves to be deeply committed believers. For them, the civil war is over. Traditionalists lost. The marvelous cathedrals built at great sacrifice by believers in the seventeenth and eighteenth centuries now stand virtually empty. At best, they are visited on Sunday by a huddled little assembly of aging Christians. The culture has been redesigned from top to bottom by secular humanists, and they did it primarily by influencing the younger and more vulnerable members of their society.

The spiritual struggle has also subsided in Western Europe. In France, Germany, Holland, and Belgium, one does not hear the great debates that rage throughout North America. The pro-life community and the anti-pornography movement are much less vocal. Likewise, an entire generation of children is growing up in those countries with no memory of Christian concepts. For them, a meaningful faith is simply outside their realm of experience. This reordering of society can be accomplished quite easily when conditions are right.

The Educational Battleground

The campaign to isolate children from their parents and to indoctrinate them with humanistic ideas is being waged primarily in the public schools, as I have indicated. I must emphasize, however, that the Judeo-Christian system of values is still very evident in many educational districts. This is what makes for bloody conflict.

As we will see, the hottest battles in this civil war are being fought on educational turf, and that is where eventual victory or defeat will occur. At this moment, the traditionalists are being mauled, but they're not yet down for the count.

My purpose in addressing these activities of the secular humanists should be apparent by this point. We cannot defend our families and the things we believe unless we are informed of the dangers.

Perhaps you remember the peace movement's slogan from the sixties that read, "What if they gave a war and nobody came?" My concern in the present day is that a war has been "given" and only one side appears to know about it. Most disturbing is the fact that many parents—perhaps the majority—appear not to really *want* to know.

That situation must change on both the national and the local levels if we are to prevail in the great Civil War of Values. There is not a moment to lose!

I indicated earlier that the secular humanists hold sway in every American center of power and influence except two, the church and the family. Furthermore, we've emphasized that these two institutions are under severe pressure and are not yet mobilized for the struggle. Under these circumstances, what hope is there that the Judeo-Christian system of thought can survive?

How can it withstand the daily hammering it takes in the press, on television, from liberal universities, from People for the American Way, from the ACLU, the National Organization for Women, the National Abortion Rights Action League, and from regular tampering by ambitious and tax-obsessed congressmen? Could even the Rock of Gibraltar withstand such a barrage? Have we already lost the great Civil War of Values? Some people seem to hope so.

A public relations firm recently issued a promotional letter that reached my desk. It touted a new novel by popular writer, Rona Jaffe, whose works have sold more than 23 million copies. Her newest book takes the position that marriage as we have known it is dying. Now-and-forever relationships are yielding to what Jaffe calls "sequential monogamy," which is tantamount to "temporary fidelity." It refers to a series of short-term hook-ups among the not-so-committed.

"Men are not only cheating on their wives," Jaffe says. "They're also cheating on their mistresses."

She then drives home the point. "In a hospital at this very moment there is a baby with your name on it who is going to grow up and take away your future husband."

The promotional letter then ends with the question, "If marriage is dying, what will happen to the family?" Fortunately, Jaffe has the answer, and is available this fall for interviews and guest appearances throughout North America. So stay tuned. Rona is coming to *your* city. Whoopee!

How about it? Are traditional, long-term, committed marriages becoming obsolete? Are we really moving toward "sequential monogamy," as Jaffe supposes? Will children of the future grow up in multiple unstable families as their mothers and fathers flit from one temporary relationship to another?

Well, a credible answer to those questions was provided shortly after the announcement of Jaffe's availability. The Gallup organization published their findings from a poll that addressed the precise issues in question.

The results were most encouraging. Ninety-two percent of those interviewed said they had never been unfaithful to their spouses. Eighty-three percent said they would marry the same partner again, if given a chance. Seventy-six percent considered their spouses to be physically attractive. Sixty-one percent of couples said they pray together as a family. And so it went. Gallup's conclusion?

Marriages today are stronger than previously believed. Sorry, Rona!

That is very good news from the home front. But there is more. *Parents* magazine reported in the January 16, 1990 issue on their poll of 1,000 people. They found that 78 percent of respondents expressed a desire to return to "traditional values and old-fashioned morality." Imagine that! After forty years of sex and violence on television, 78 percent of us still recognize that evil is evil and must not be embraced.

A Moral Victory

I'm encouraged to report that hope *does* thrive, and that it emanates from the collective wisdom of the American people. We should never underestimate the ability of our countrymen to choose between good and bad alternatives. This characteristic has prevailed within us for nearly 300 years, going back to the influence of the Puritans and the framers of the U.S. Constitution.

My friend, Charlie Jarvis, observed that our godly forefathers acted as though they had swallowed "gyroscopes" that helped them distinguish between right and wrong. Their behavior and their public policy decisions seemed to have been guided by what they believed to have been a divinely inspired sense of direction. That is why offices of government in England were called "ministries"— reflecting this deeply felt moral foundation for everything the Puritans believed.

Those internal gyroscopes still operate deep within the spirits of the American people. The majority of us carry a memory of our Christian heritage, even though every effort has been made to extinguish and ridicule it.

It is most evident in our generosity toward the disadvantaged and the wounded in our midst. Just last Sunday afternoon, my wife and I visited my elderly aunt in the nursing home where she is confined. When we arrived, an informal church service was in progress.

A family of six, including two children, had come to the institution to sing and share the Scriptures with the sick and dying patients. Arrayed in front of them were about twenty white-haired, aged women slumped in their wheel chairs. Most were senile or too weak to respond. It made no difference. The young family had come to comfort and entertain them with music and truths from God's Word.

I stood watching from the doorway and struggled to hold back the tears. I felt a great love for this little band of servants who had given their time unselfishly to care for such a pitiful flock of women who could not even express their appreciation. Though I did not know the singers, I thanked God for the compassion and kindness I heard in their voices.

This, I thought, represents the *best* of the Christian ethic. Sure, we've heard about a few ministers visiting prostitutes and absconding with God's money. The media flood us with the details when Christians fail. But there is another side. It will not be told in the newspapers tomorrow morning. It is a story of kindness and love expressed by caring people in countless quiet ways.

I wondered as I stood in that nursing home where the secular humanists were that afternoon. Those would-be rescuers claim to have such great interest in the poor and the victimized when they come to Washington in search of federal grants. But who do you find working among the wretched, the sick and the powerless when there is not one thin dime to be gained in return?

Typically, it will be those with deeply-felt spiritual commitments who give themselves unreservedly to people in need. Why do they do it? Because the Master told them to.

This is the heritage of faith that thrives within the breasts of countless millions around the world. They are the salt of the earth, and without their influence, the social order would quickly degenerate into chaos. And you can believe this: those quiet, godly people care passionately for their children.

They have permitted their sons and daughters to come under the influence of immoral, atheistic bureaucrats and educators because they've been too busy to notice. But when the necessary information is given to them, I believe they will rise up to defend the beliefs and values that were handed to them by their ancestors! They will not long tolerate the destruction of everything they hold dear. I would stake my life on that certainty.

The Counterattack

If *you* are among the body of concerned citizens, I urge you not to just sit there. Get out and work for what you believe. Democracy only succeeds when people get involved. Campaign for a position on the local school board. Write your representatives in Washington. Better yet, help elect congressmen and senators who hold to the Judeo-Christian system of values.

Picket an abortion clinic. Serve on the hospital lay committee. Take a teacher to dinner. Examine the policies of your local library. Support your neighborhood crisis pregnancy center. Accept a pregnant teenager into your home. Write the producers and sponsors of sex and violence on television. Petition the city council to rid your town of adult bookstores and dirty theaters. Pray for your country every day. Support the work of your church in reaching a lost and dying world for Christ. And by all means, do these things in a spirit of love that would be honoring to the One who sent us.

Where will the time and energy be found to make America "family-friendly" again? I don't know. Warfare has always been exhausting, dangerous, and expensive. But how can we remain uninvolved when the welfare of our children and subsequent generations is on the line? That is the question of the hour.

3

LOVE AND SEX

In any major conflict between two established armies, a bloody collision will eventually occur that proves to be decisive. Forever after, historians will remember that terrible struggle as the turning point—as the battle that made the difference.

For Napoleon, the turning point was Waterloo. It was Stalingrad and Normandy for Hitler. It was Midway for the Japanese. It was Gettysburg and Vicksburg for the Confederate Army. Those were the bloody battlegrounds that largely determined, not only victory or defeat in a particular campaign, but the ultimate outcome of the war.

It appears that we are engaged in that kind of struggle in the current Civil War of Values. The hottest and most dangerous confrontation to date—and the battle that may well establish the eventual winner—is being fought over child and adolescent sexuality and the policies relevant to it.

It is here that secular humanists have made their most audacious invasion of the homeland. It is here that every cherished ideal and belief in the Judeo-Christian system of values has been assaulted. And it is here that slumbering

traditionalists have awakened to find themselves surrounded and their children captured by the amoralists on
the other side. Look at what has been lost in a few brief
years. Virginity is a joke. Premarital sex is the norm. Ten
and twelve year-olds talk openly about oral sex and the
most intimate adult subjects. Dial-a-porn has invaded their
childish world. Homosexuality has become a "valid"
lifestyle with protected minority status.

Traditional teachings of the church are contradicted
daily in the classroom. Parents have lost the right even to
know when their daughters have aborted a baby. Condoms
are distributed willy-nilly by school officials. Venereal disease is rampant. Language is so foul it is even decried by
the *secular* press. Ultimately, the faith for which parents
would give their lives is undermined and weakened among
the young. It's all here! Again I say, this is the theater of war
that will establish the course of Western civilization for
centuries to come. And we are losing it!

Why, we might ask, have the secular humanists chosen
child and adolescent sexuality as the battleground on
which to press their advantage? Why have they been so
aggressive at this particular point, blatantly contradicting
what they know to be the most deeply held convictions and
ideologies of Christians and conservatives? For some good
reasons, I assure you.

First, by teaching children an entirely different sexual ethic than their parents hold, a wedge is driven between generations that makes kids vulnerable to other
alien ideas.

Second, there is no better way to destroy the family
than to undermine the sexual exclusivity on which life-long
marriage is based. And, as we have seen, if the family collapses, the heartland of the nation is wide open to cultural
revolution.

Third, premarital chastity and marital monogamy are
centerpieces of nearly all major religions. To destroy these
ancient concepts in the minds of today's children is to

weaken or totally negate their faith. Imagine, for example, a 15 year-old boy or girl sitting in church on Sunday morning after having clandestine intercourse the night before. The contradiction between behavior and belief will produce discomfort, leading either to repentance—or to withdrawal from the source of guilt. The latter is more common.

Rejecting Moral Traditions

The aim of the humanists is to cause young people in every area of our culture to reject the moral traditions which have always undergirded this society. James Hitchcock says it best:

> . . . certain proponents of the sexual revolution therefore know exactly what they are doing when they promote it, for they realize that if people of traditional values can be made to change their minds (not even necessarily their behavior) on this matter, they will prove easily malleable in other areas as well. The assault on traditional Christian sexual morality is an attempt to shatter all deeply held, uncompromisable moral convictions, to make people into perfectly mobile, infinitely manipulable creatures.[1]

Children, of course, can be the easiest to manipulate and mold into a "new creature." As Hitchcock notes, sexual behavior is very close to the heart of one's personality. How we behave sexually, perhaps even more than how we think about how we behave, does a great deal to define who we are.

Mary Calderone, one of the gurus of the modern sex education movement, admitted a similar point. She said the purpose of these programs is not merely to tell kids about the birds and bees. It is to reorder their minds. As she put it,

> If man, as he is, is obsolescent, then what kind do we want to produce in his place and how do we design the production line? That is the real question facing . . . sex education.[2]

That is a surprisingly frank expression of secular humanistic intentions. Society as it has been—with its Judeo-Christian origins—must be redesigned and reconstructed. There is only one way to accomplish a feat of that magnitude, and that is to isolate kids from their parents and reprogram their values.

Sex, therefore, is the hydrogen bomb that permits the destruction of things as they are and a simultaneous reconstruction of the new order. As Calderone says, "Human beings of the brave new world will be 'consciously engineered' by societies' best minds, who will provide for the necessary conditioning."

Parents! Are you listening? Those are *your* children Calderone plans to re-engineer! Are you willing to turn them over to this woman and her colleagues? I pray not!

That is the background for the abominable programs now operating in public schools under the rubric of sex education. The threat of AIDS has been used as a battering ram to force these avant-garde classes into the curriculum —continuing in some cases from kindergarten to grade 12. As early as 1980, only one-third of our kids had been through sex ed in the public schools. By 1989, that figure was three-fourths.[3]

If parents fully understood what is being taught in the most extreme situations, they would be outraged. Imagine, for example, seventh grade boys and girls sitting in co-ed programs that requires them to slide condoms on and off bananas. In one school, I'm told, they even exhibited a plastic model of an erect penis.

Education to Excess

Recently a student and his parent who visited our Focus on the Family headquarters offered to report the curriculum used in a psychology class at a high school in Newport Beach, California.

The teacher allegedly exposed his class of co-ed sophomores to virtually every known perversion, from bestiality
between horses and women, to eroticism with excrement.
He also covered other subjects in such detail that I would
not describe them in this book.

Subsequently there was the usual visit from homosexual activists, presenting—and promoting—their lifestyles
to wide-eyed sophomores. This kind of information has a
dramatic effect on the minds of impressionable fifteen year-
old male and female students. I don't care how liberated we
have become. That is unconscionable!

Most parents never have an opportunity to examine
the curriculum taught in sex-ed classes. I took a detailed
look at some of the typical programs several years ago,
after I received a volume of material from a member of the
White House staff. He had been asked to investigate how
educators are approaching the topic, and he was shocked
by what he learned. I shared his alarm.

Provided below are the concepts *commonly* taught in
public schools today. (I must alert you that the following
materials are highly explicit. Read the next page or two
only if you really want to know!) If it offends you, how do
you feel about your children reading similar concepts in
class?

1. As might be expected, premarital sex is routinely
promoted, with efforts made to reduce guilt, inhibitions,
moral imperatives and prior teachings. Abstinence is
mocked or made to look hopelessly out of date.

One text, *Boys and Sex* by Wardell B. Pomeroy, basically provides a "how to" description for male sexual conquest.[4] A lengthy paragraph is provided describing fondling
and sucking of breasts, touching of the genitals, placing the
mouth on the girl's vagina, putting the penis in the girl's
mouth, etc. Then Pomeroy writes, "Some girls may draw
the line at one point or another in the progression I've
described, but most people engage in all of this behavior

before marriage." Finally he states, "Consequently, petting is fun . . . for both boys and girls . . ."

In the companion book, *Girls and Sex*, Pomeroy lists "reasons why a girl might think favorably of having intercourse for the first time."[5] What follows is a cleverly written rationale for going all the way. It is addressed exclusively to young girls and points out how much fun sex is, how helpful premarital intercourse is in preparing for marriage, ("there are many girls who regret after marriage that they didn't have premarital intercourse") and how much faster one learns when young. These books are published by Delacorte Press, a division of Bantam Books, and are widely used in schools today!

2. Desensitization techniques are used to make the subject of sex more familiar and commonplace. Gutter language is quoted and discussed. One workbook sent by the White House provided a ten-inch rectangular box and instructed the student to "Draw the World's Largest Penis." The caption read, "If I had the world's largest penis . . . make up a wild story."

A true or false test, entitled "All About Cocks and Balls and Things," presented these kind of questions, "Black dicks are always larger?" and "Blue balls come from not coming?" and other such vulgar jokes. Crude cartoon drawings were shown of copulating couples, and then the assignment was given to "draw mother and father making love." Another assignment instructed the students not to forget "grandfather's asshole."

3. Concern over homosexuality and lesbianism is presented as a myth and fallacy. These perversions are typically held up as valid lifestyles. Pomeroy's book, *Girls and Sex*, actually encourages girls who sleep at a female friend's house to stimulate each other to orgasm. "Everyone has homosexual tendencies in one degree or another," he says.

4. Marriage receives a consistent, but subtle, drubbing. Various alternatives, from living together to communal and

group marriages, are offered as options for consideration. The authors go to great lengths to show that there is no good or bad behavior—nothing really right or wrong.

This point is made emphatically. Everything is relevant. What's best for *you* is what counts. But you can be sure that the dangers of early sexual behavior are never presented, however, making it difficult for kids to understand the true implications. The only consideration is doing things "right" . . . that is, with contraceptives and "proper protection."

5. Societal attitudes based on the Christian ethic are universally undermined, such as opposition to legalized prostitution, "saving oneself till marriage," etc.

6. The authors are not satisfied with explaining *normal* sexual experiences. The programs often include an emphasis on behavior that many adults would not experience in a lifetime, such as sex with various animals, same-sex encounters, anal intercourse, sex with excrement, on and on.

7. Contraceptives are distributed and discussed in class. One teacher's guide published by the U.S. Government says, "The rubber usually attracts a lot of giggles and the teens like to experiment with the foam. They also like to insert the diaphragm in the model and remove it."

Moral Outrage

I don't mind telling you that material of this nature makes me very angry. It is designed to subvert the minds of vulnerable kids, including those whose parents hold tightly to Christian concepts and morality. The thought of atheistic and immoral teachers presenting this kind of tripe in a public school classroom—especially if my kid were sitting there—is absolutely intolerable to me.

What in the name of common sense do we *expect* kids to do after they've been granted such license? *Of course* they will use it! They are only 13 to 17 years of age, for Pete's sake. They've just been given the most exciting information in the history of the world, and then they're told there are no overriding moral principles involved in using it. The only question is, "Are you ready?"

Are you kidding? I've seen very few teenage boys who didn't think they were *ready!* They may or may not choose to remember what they were taught about contraceptives, but they will *never* forget what they learned about those wonderful female creatures around them.

There is another aspect of this sensory bombardment that concerns me. Highly explicit sex ed programs of this nature are particularly dangerous because they shred the natural modesty between the sexes which is designed to protect them from premature sexual experience. This is especially true for girls. After the amoralists stop laughing at such a comment, they have to come to grips with the phenomenon of date rape, which is rampant now in high schools and colleges.

Doctoral student, Ginny Sandberg, at the University of South Dakota, found that 20 percent of coeds she interviewed had been raped during a dating situation. That led *Ms.* magazine to conduct its own investigation directed by psychologist Mary K. Koss from Kent State University. Their findings, based on interviews with 7,000 women from 35 U.S. universities, revealed that one quarter of the female students have been victims of rape or attempted rape.

Ninety percent knew their assailants. Koss said, "One of every eight women were victims of rape according to the prevailing legal definition. Forty-seven percent of the rapes were by first or casual dates or by romantic acquaintances. Three-quarters of the women raped were between the ages of 15–21. The average age at the time of the rape was 18. More than 80 percent of the rapes occurred off campus— with more than 50 percent on the man's turf—his home, car or other. More than 90 percent of the women raped did not tell the police."[6]

This is the nightmare we have created with our sexual liberation and with our Calderone-type reprogramming in the classroom. It has been a social disaster. Everyone with an open mind must acknowledge that fact by now.

The incidence of pregnancy, abortion and disease is heading through the roof. We must put a stop to these humanistic curricula, but only parents can get that accomplished. Unfortunately, moms and dads are often too busy to notice. Or, more understandably, they don't know how to buck the system.

You can't blame Dad for being a little queasy about taking on the establishment. He's thinking, "I sure don't want to make a fool of myself in the community. That wouldn't help my son or daughter. After all, look at all the pros on the other side. My goodness! There are educators, psychologists, physicians, counselors and teachers who think this is a wonderful thing. And who am I? Just a hung-up reactionary, I guess. I don't think I can stand up to all that brass. Besides, if what is happening is so terrible, where are the other parents who disagree? I must be the only one who's nervous about what is being taught. Maybe *I'm* crazy."

Then Phil Donahue airs a television program featuring a panel of magnificent experts lined up against a diminutive, balding, unprepared, inarticulate, and uneducated representative of the Christian view, and the secular experts eat his lunch. That does it. The parent tiptoes away.

Others just don't ask. They don't investigate! They just close their eyes and hope. They hope that someone will use a little common sense in what is taught. That leaves the door wide open to the hearts of the kids.

Confounding the Experts

With the evidence growing that early sexual involvement should be discouraged, some school districts have tried to reinstitute common sense and a value basis to the issue of teen sexuality. Unfortunately, they often become targets for outraged ACLU attorneys.

In the State of Washington, for example, administrators in a local district adopted an outstanding sex and AIDS education curriculum based on abstinence. The two programs "Teen Aid" and "Sex Respect" are widely used in other school districts around the country and were developed and shown to be effective with grants from the federal government.

Despite this national acceptance, the State Superintendent's office ruled that the district violated state regulations because their material acknowledged only the traditional family, gave limited information on contraception, was written from the pro-life perspective, and was presented strictly within the context of marriage.

It is difficult to believe that those time-honored concepts could be declared illegal today, given their significance in our cultural history. If I lived in the State of Washington, you can be sure that I would be campaigning for a new Superintendent of Instruction and a more conservative slate of legislators.

In Chesapeake, Virginia, school officials wrote and distributed a classroom brochure in an attempt to promote chastity. Unfortunately, they made a fatal mistake. The brochure said, with no apology, "God has given each person a priceless gift, but many people carelessly give it away."

You can guess what happened next. A lawyer in a three-piece suit from the ACLU threatened to take legal action unless that terrible word "God" was removed from the literature! The Chesapeake School Board Chairman summarized the situation accurately when he said, "Isn't it terrible when you attempt to teach what's right and wrong and another group takes a stance that you can't tell kids what's right and wrong?" Yes, it is terrible and absurd. Ultimately our children, and our nation, will suffer from their foolishness.

Higher Ed Takes The Low Road

If sex education programs in elementary and secondary schools are troublesome for parents, I wonder if they know what the college and university scene is like today. Take a look at what the "graduates" of public school sex education programs are thinking, now that they're in college. They learned their lessons well.

The parents of a freshman girl at UCLA. told me recently of the enormous pressure she is under to surrender her virginity. All of her friends and sorority sisters are not only "sexually active," but some are involved in multiple experiences in a single night. This girl has found no one she respects who is holding to a standard of morality.

Another family with a daughter attending a Midwestern university said the girl is unable to date, because among her associates, to date is to go to bed with the escort. Furthermore, on Wednesday evenings, free beer is provided to all dorm residents. Many of the students become drunk every week, fouling their living quarters and behaving like animals.

Is this kind of behavior unique to the schools I have mentioned? Of course not. It is typical of life on most university campuses today.

A female student at Stanford University sent me a copy of the campus newspaper, *Stanford Review*. The headline touted the university's recently sponsored "Condom Rating Contest" in which students were asked to evaluate seven different condoms on the basis of "smell, taste, appearance, sensualness/comfort, lubrication, and sense of security." A pamphlet included with the condom packages encouraged students to "try out these condoms by yourself, with a partner, or partners. Be creative. Have fun. Enjoy."

At the Claremont Colleges, also in California, a full schedule of hilarious activities was planned for National Condom Awareness Week. They included glow-in-the-dark condoms on sale for $1.00; a sale of condoms clipped to Valentines for exchange between students; a "Condom Couplet Contest" where the object was to invent a rhyme to be quoted to someone refusing to wear a condom.

They also planned a "Condom Olympics," which included a water filled condom toss, and an event called "Pin The Condom on the Man." A photograph in the school paper featured a smiling young lady shown holding a banana on which she was unrolling a condom.

Thank God for one faculty member, Dr. Henry Jaffa, who objected to the frivolity. He wrote,

> Nearly everyone knows . . . that the family is rooted in man's and woman's love of their own. And love of one's own is rooted in the exclusiveness of the sexual passion. A man's confidence in his wife's chastity is the foundation of their family. And the integrity of the family is the foundation of all human well-being in society. Promiscuity on campuses may be looked upon either as an inescapable reality or as the latest fad . . . like goldfish swallowing. But it is an almost certain guarantee that all, or nearly all, of the marriages ensuing will end in divorce, and in pain and suffering . . . above all for women and children. That the silly banana handlers of today can hardly imagine.[7]

Perhaps it is now evident why child and adolescent sexuality are seen as critical to the survival of the Judeo-Christian ethic, and indeed, to the continuance of Western civilization itself. We human beings are sexual creatures. God made us that way. We recognize our sex assignment as boys or girls from our earliest moments of self-awareness, and that identification will influence everything we do to the end of our lives.

It is impossible to overstate the influence of this sexual nature in understanding ourselves and our social interactions. And as Dr. Jaffa indicated, it provides the basis for the bond that holds a man and woman in committed union. The permanence of that relationship then provides an environment in which the next generation can grow and flourish.

Legitimate Expression

It follows, then, that stability in society is dependent on the healthy expression of our sexual nature. If this energy within us is siphoned off in the pursuit of pleasure; if it is squandered in non-exclusive relationships; if it is perverted in same-sex activities, then the culture is deprived of the working, saving, sacrificing, caring, building, growing, reproducing units known as families.

Robbed of sexual standards, society will unravel like a ball of twine. That is the lesson of history. That is the legacy of Rome and more than 2,000 civilizations that have come and gone on this earth. The family is the basic unit of society on which all human activity rests. If you tamper with the sexual nature of familial relationships, you necessarily threaten the entire superstructure. Indeed, ours is swaying like a drunken sailor from the folly of our cultural engineers.

Finally, there is this to say about child and adolescent sexuality. What is at stake here is nothing less than the *faith* of our children. Our ultimate objective in living must be the spiritual welfare of our sons and daughters. If we lose it there, we have lost everything.

But isn't that just the point? The kind of sex education program now operating in America's schools is *designed* as a crash course in relativism, in immorality, and in anti-Christian philosophy. And it has been remarkably successful in recasting the social order.

We must reassert ourselves in public education and reintroduce the value system that made this country great. How can we continue to sit back and watch our philosophical opponents reprogram our children?

James C. Dobson

4

QUESTIONS AND ANSWERS

When I have spoken publicly about the concern presented in the previous three chapters, I have typically been greeted by a flurry of related questions from the audience. Applying that format, I think it would be appropriate at this point to respond to some of the common questions I am asked.

Q: I read recently that the definition of the family needed to be revised in light of cultural changes. The writer said a family should be thought of as "a circle of love," including any individuals who were deeply attached to each other. Somehow, I know this is wrong but can't articulate why. How do you see it?

A: I am familiar with the effort to redefine the family. It is motivated by homosexual activists and others who see this institution as a barrier to the social engineering they hope to accomplish.

But what is the traditional definition of the family? It is a group of individuals who are related to one another by marriage, birth, or adoption—nothing more, nothing else. The family was divinely instituted and sanctioned in the beginning, when God created one man and one woman, brought them together, and commanded them to "be fruitful and multiply." This is where we begin and this is where we must stand.

By contrast, if by "family" we mean any circle of people who love each other, then the term ceases to have meaning. In that case, five homosexual men can be a "family" until one feels unloved, and then there are four.

Under such a definition, one man and six women could be regarded as a legal entity, reintroducing the debate over polygamy. We thought we settled that one in the last century.

It would also be possible for parents who dislike a rebellious teenager to opt him out of the "circle of love," thus depriving him of any legal identity with the family. Under these amorphous terms, wives would have no greater legal protection than female acquaintances with whom men become infatuated. We end up with an unstable social structure rife with potential for disaster.

There is good reason, then, to defend the narrow legal definition of the family as understood over the centuries. After all, the family as I have characterized it is not merely human in origin. It is God's marvelous creation. And He has not included casual social relationships—even the most loving ones—within that bond of kinship. Nor should we.

Q: You cited some of the objectives the secular humanists hope to accomplish in America. Would you list their other ideas and educational goals?

A: I have been interested in that question for several years. By reading the press and monitoring the media, it has been possible, I think, to identify a host of objectives that might be called "the family agenda of the left." Listed below are their goals as I perceive them.

1. Convince the public that the training and development of children are far too important to be left to the whims and errors of parents. Only child-development authorities and professionals, commissioned by the government, can do the job properly. Mothers and fathers must yield control to those who are better equipped for the task of raising children.

2. Propagandize heavily against the use of corporal punishment as a disciplinary measure with children. Equate it with child abuse, even when administered judiciously by loving parents. Ultimately, secure legislation to outlaw the practice.

3. Continually emphasize an exhaustive list of "children's rights," which will provide wedges to separate kids from their parents.

4. Provide mandatory schooling for every four year-old, so that young minds can be controlled. This will be accomplished first through government-sponsored child care centers. Once established with federal funds, they should eventually drive unassisted church-based facilities out of competition.

5. Teach students that gay and lesbian lifestyles are no less moral than heterosexual relationships, and that they typically involve long-term monogamous commitments. Teach girls that it is just as appropriate to fall in love and have intimate relationships with another girl as with a boy (and do the same for boys). Design counseling programs for gay and lesbian students that will permit subtle recruitment services. (This is being done in Los

Angeles City Schools through a program called Project 10. It *assumes* that ten percent of students are homosexual, and provides programs to recruit and support new converts.)

6. Demystify the occult. Shirley MacLaine has assisted immeasurably here. *Any* belief system other than the Christian faith is seen as an improvement, including the mysticism of Eastern religions.

7. Remove all references to God from school literature, such as with regard to the Pilgrims' worship on Thanksgiving, and from every dimension of public life.

8. Work to remove tax exemptions for religious institutions and begin to control them through regulatory and legislative mandate.

9. Require churches, businesses, and schools to hire gays, lesbians and others who contradict their faith.

10. Promote Gay-Pride celebrations in every American city, and seek equivalent legal status of families for homosexual and lesbian partners.

11. Expand the power of government and its bureaucracies to control every vestige of private life.

12. Increase the tax burden on families, forcing more women into the work force and their children into child care facilities.

13. Require military women to fight in combat.

14. Repeal all laws relating to obscenity, and even child pornography.

15. Eliminate the motion picture rating system so that patrons (and parents) cannot easily avoid violent and explicit sexuality in films.

16. Make homemakers feel exploited, stupid and useless. Especially at the college and university level, ridicule female students who wish to marry, to have a family, or to postpone or avoid a career.

17. Oppose with vengeance any effort to teach, or

even mention, creation as an explanation for the earth's beginnings.

18. Monitor every judge appointed or seeking election. The judiciary is *the* key to the leftist agenda.

19. Secure far-reaching rights of students on junior and senior high school campuses. Limit the authority of teachers and principals to enforce rules of conduct.

20. Implement an aggressive sex-ed program, beginning in kindergarten, that is guided by no moral code. Safe-sex is its centerpiece.

21. Provide for legal infanticide in cases of severe handicap or mental retardation.

22. Guarantee the "right to die" to anyone desiring suicide. Physicians should be free to assist in the act of dying.

23. Work to remove all state sodomy laws.

24. Fight tooth and nail to retain the right to abortion on demand—up to the moment of birth—for any reason whatsoever.

25. Operate aggressive "death education" classes in public schools to desensitize children to dying and to help them see life materialistically.

There are other objectives, I'm sure, but these appear to be the most pressing.

Q: When I've tried to argue the "abstinence" position with the advocates of "safe sex," they have said, "You just don't live in the real world. Kids are going to do what comes naturally. It is ridiculous to ask them to abstain, so we might as well show them how to do it right." Is it hopeless to teach principles of morality to this generation?

A: I've heard the same hopelessness from the advocates of safe-sex. They don't *want* kids to abstain, so they tell us it is foolish to promote that behavior. Nothing could be farther from the truth.

I remember a reporter from the *New York Times* coming to Focus on the Family last year to get a quote from us. She was writing a story about today's sexually active kids, making the point that morality is dead and gone. We disagreed and invited her to come to Lexington, Kentucky, to attend a youth rally we were co-sponsoring with local ministries. It featured ex-convict Harold Morris, who gave teenagers straight talk about sex, drugs, their choice of friends, and other concerns. The reporter accepted our invitation and was blown away by what she saw. The stadium was designed to hold only 18,000 people, but 26,000 kids showed up for the rally. Several thousand who couldn't get inside stood listening to a speaker system outside the arena as Harold told them to stay out of bed until they are married.

The reporter went back to New York and—you guessed it—wrote that morality is dead among the young. It isn't true. But it *will* be soon if we continue to slumber.

Q: Do you really believe parents are interested in national trends that affect their children and families? If so, why aren't they more involved?

A: I'm convinced that they *care* passionately about their children and the things that affect them. They will fight to their last breath to repel any threat to those they love. The issue, then, is not one of commitment. The problem is a matter of stress and exhaustion. Most of us in North America live every day on the ragged edge, holding down multiple jobs and running full tilt from morning to night. There is simply nothing left with which to cope. Surviving another day takes priority over governmental concerns or even subtle trends in local school districts. We do well to even vote in general elections. Surveys show that only one to two percent of the population ever bother to write a letter to a public official. We just don't have the time or energy. Thus, our breathless pace creates a vacuum into which the social engineers and revolutionaries take residence. By the time we notice what is going on, another component of traditional family life has been undermined.

Q: If Americans are so disinterested in what is going on nationally, why is the network news so prominent on radio and television each morning and night?

A: The fact is, the network news is far less influential today than it was a decade ago. Fewer people are watching and less detail is given. What used to be comprehensive coverage of national events has now become more or less a headline service, much like the shallow, inch-deep reporting in *USA Today.*

Let me illustrate. About a year ago, the general manager for radio station KFWB in Los Angeles came by my office. We enjoyed an interesting conversation, during which I asked him why his all-news format did not focus more attention on national events?

"That's not what our listeners want," he replied.

He went on to tell me that according to careful polling of his constituency, he learned that they listen to his station to obtain information in the following order: (1) time; (2) weather; (3) traffic; (4) local events; and finally, (5) national news. That about tells the story.

In the absence of public scrutiny and interest, our governmental leaders have been able to ignore the interest of families and implement, instead, policies that benefit activists and single-minded special interest groups.

Q: **Why are people who believe in traditonal values less involved in public issues than the secular humanists? Do people who hold the Judeo-Christian system of values care less about their ideas than the liberals do?**

A: I have been troubled by that question for several years. Most of the Christians I know would die for their faith if necessary, and yet they consistently get whipped in the public arena. Their philosophical opponents get there first, fight better when the heat is on, and remain on the battlefield after the pro-family people have gone home. How can this be? Why is our army so tentative?

After giving the matter much thought, I believe I now understand the problem. *The other side earns a living by winning these battles, while we are merely motivated by ideology.* Anti-family organizations receive multiplied millions of dollars in subsidies each year. It is no wonder they fight like fanatics for those funds in Washington.

Likewise, the abortionists, the pornographers, the educators and the empire-building bureaucrats all feed at the public trough. Their livelihood *depends* on personal involvement in government. Our side has no such motivation. As I've indicated, we're up to our ears in responsibility at home. If it requires a major sacrifice just to fight a quick battle or two, most of us apparently find it too costly to get involved.

This economic reality helps to explain the tenacity of the left on such issues as the Equal Rights Amendment. They don't give up, even after years of defeat and disappointment. Look at the child care issue. The humanists fought for government-sponsored babysitting for 20 years without success, continually chipping away at the opposition. Finally, public opinion began to swing their way.

How about our ground troops? We get discouraged and embarrassed by a single setback. Remember the Civil Rights Restoration Act of 1988, which stands as Congress' most serious assault on religious liberty? More than one million people called or wrote their representatives to complain in two days, blowing switchboards and jamming telephone lines for an entire section of the city.

The result? Congressmen and senators ignored their opposition, and not a one of them was forced to pay for the insult during the next election. In fact, Congress has a higher rate of incumbency than the Politburo in Moscow. Why? Because Christians have a very short memory and the politicians know it.

Obviously, we must learn to go the distance if we're to have a chance at victory. Votes are what it's all about, and yet, half the Christians are not even registered! No wonder we get whipped year in and out.

Q: What role is rock music playing in the pressure we're seeing on this generation of teenagers?

A: It is difficult to overestimate the negative impact music is having. Rock stars are the heroes, the idols, that young people want to emulate. And when they are depicted in violent and sexual roles, many teenagers and pre-adolescents are pulled along in their wake.

What could possibly be wholesome about showing explicit sexual scenes—especially those involving perversions—to 12 and 13 year-old kids? Yet videos come into the home via MTV and other channels that feature men and women in blatantly sexual situations, or even in depictions of sadism.

One study showed that more than half of all MTV videos featured violence or implied violence, and 35 percent revealed violence against women. A steady diet of this garbage will pollute the minds of even the healthiest of teenagers.

I believe that this perpetual and pernicious exposure to rock music is responsible, at least in part, for many of the social problems now occurring among the young, including the high suicide rate, the reported willingness of young men to rape women if given an opportunity, and the moral undermining of the next generation.

As a case in point, you may remember the flap that occurred in 1990 over the rap group 2 Live Crew, and their album, "As Nasty As They Wanna Be." A Florida judge reviewed the filthy lyrics of this album and, for the first time ever, a judicial official declared a piece of "music" to be obscene and illegal.

Predictably, Phil Donahue and his cronies in the press threw their usual temper tantrums when the news broke. "Censorship!" they cried from the rooftops. Virtually every newspaper in the country carried editorials and feature stories about the audacity of the judge who imposed his standard of morality on the rest of us.

Dan Rather, on his show "48 Hours," made the most outlandish statements about our loss of freedoms in this era of oppression. And Geraldo Rivera risked getting his nose broken again by bringing 2 Live Crew and their critics face-to-face on his television show.

What the media did not tell the American people, however, was the content of 2 Live Crew's album. They *censored* that information from the public, choosing instead to talk abstractly about "First Amendment Rights" and "right-wing fundamentalists." Does that seem a bit strange to you?

Millions of words were spoken about the obscene lyrics to a single album, yet no one would quote them directly. Why not? Because adults would be shocked and outraged by their filth and debauchery. Thus, language which was unfit to print or utter on television was considered perfectly acceptable for the consumption of young minds. That is the logic of Phil, Dan and Geraldo.

At the risk of upsetting our readers, let me list for you—as discreetly as possible—the words that appeared in the one album, "As Nasty As They Wanna Be." They included:

- 226 uses of the "F" -word
- 117 explicit terms for male or female genitalia
- 87 descriptions of oral sex
- 163 uses of the word for female dog
- 15 uses of "ho" (slang for whore) when referring to women
- 81 uses of the vulgarity "s—t"
- 42 uses of the word "ass"
- 9 descriptions of male ejaculation
- 6 references to erections
- 4 descriptions of group sex
- 3 mentions of rimming (oral/anal sex)
- 2 inclusions of urination or feces
- 1 reference to incest
- over a dozen illustrations of violent sex

Please understand that these words did not appear singularly in the album. They were used to describe specific acts and attitudes. Remember, too, that youngsters buying this "music"—some only eight to ten years of age—typically listened to it dozens of times.

Descriptions of oral sex and extreme violence against women were thereby memorized and burned into the conscious experience of kids barely out of elementary school. More than two million albums were sold, and with the exception of Florida and a few other locations where it was banned, no restrictions were placed on its distribution. A child of any age could purchase it.

This is merely one salvo in an industry that has helped to destroy the moral code of Western civilization. It has been accomplished methodically and deliberately during the past thirty years, in cooperation with television and movie producers. The damage has been incalculable!

I feel like the patriarch, Lot, when he said of Sodom and Gomorrah more than 4,000 years ago: I am "vexed with the filthy conversation of the wicked" (2 Peter 2:7 KJV).

Q: I don't believe kids are as easily influenced as you say. What they see does not necessarily determine how they behave.

A: Well, look at it this way. Do you remember when the movie *ET* was the rage back in 1982? There was a brief scene in the film where the extra-terrestrial was given a few pieces of the candy, Reese's Pieces. The brand was not named, but children recognized it during its few seconds on the screen. In the months that followed, the sale of Reese's Pieces went through the sky. Isn't that a clear example of a movie's influence on childrens' thinking? Why do advertisers spend billions of dollars to put their products before the people if what we see and hear does not influence our behavior? Why do schools and colleges purchase textbooks for children and young adults if what they read does not translate into influence of one form or another? *Of course* they are vulnerable to what they witness! We all are. How much greater impact is made by dramatic, sexually oriented, no-holds-barred musical and theatrical presentations that are aimed at the hearts and souls of our kids?

Who are we kidding when we say they are not harmed by the worst of it?

Q: **Tell me why you support Operation Rescue, which violates trespassing laws in order to block the entrance to abortion clinics? Isn't this a contradiction of scriptural precepts?**

A: I don't think so. It is true that Christians are instructed in scripture to obey civil laws and those in authority over us. But we are also commanded to "Rescue those who are unjustly sentenced to death. . ." (Proverbs 24:11 TLB).

I believe the higher calling here would be clear if we *really* believed our own rhetoric. Are the abortionists killing babies or aren't they? That is the issue before us. To illustrate the point, let's suppose the euthanasia movement catches on in days ahead, making it legal for parents to decide whether or not they wish to continue raising their children. Suppose they could take any child under five years of age to a "Life Clinic," where the boy or girl could be put to sleep. Suppose children were walking in the front door of clinics and going out the back in coffins.

If such a horrible day ever dawned, what do you think the response of Christians would be? Would they thumb carefully through the pages of scripture to find justification for their civil disobedience? Of course not! The moral issue would be so clear that "trespassing" to prevent the killing would be of no relevance.

The murdering of innocent children would be so abhorrent to what we know of God's nature that many of us would give our lives to rescue the little ones. In a very real sense, we are confronted by that same issue today. We *are* killing babies, although we can't see them or wrap our arms around them.

I simply do not understand why some Christian leaders, whom I respect, continue to split hairs over subtle scriptural understandings, wondering whether there is a real difference between Daniel's civil disobedience and the insignificant act of trespassing by today's rescuers.

To those Christians who feel prohibited from stepping across a property line to save a baby, I would ask how long it has been since you have exceeded the speed limit in your car? Do you conform to every other minor civil ordinance in the progress of your day?

Or a better question, what would you have done as a citizen of Germany in the Second World War? The Nazi extermination camps were "legal." Would you have broken their unjust laws in order to protect unfortunate Jews? Was Corrie ten Boom's father in violation of scripture for protecting Jews from these murderers?

Certainly not! Nor are the Operation Rescue participants in violation of any moral law, in my opinion. They seek to prevent violence against a powerless minority, and that is a principle supported throughout scripture.

Q: Give us, then, a statement of your position on civil disobedience in the prevention of abortions.

A: *Life* magazine asked me that same question a few years ago, and I prepared the following statement for them. They chose to publish only a sentence or two out of context, leaving uncertainty in the mind of the reader. Here is the position in its entirety:

After World War II, German citizens living around Nazi extermination camps were required to visit the facilities to witness the atrocities they had permitted to occur. Though it was technically "legal" to kill Jews and other political prisoners, the citizens were blamed for not breaking the law in deference to a higher moral code. This is the way we feel about the slaughter of 25 million unborn children. Some of them are being burned to death by a salt solution only days before normal delivery would have occurred. This is a moral outrage that transcends the law which sanitizes the killings. We are law-abiding people and do not advocate violence or obscene and disrespectful behavior, but to be sure, we *will* follow that higher moral code nonviolently, to rescue innocent, defenseless babies. And someday, the moral issues involved here will be as clear to the world as the Nazi holocaust is today.

Q: Why is there such concern about the euthanasia movement? If a sick, elderly person wants to die with dignity, I don't see why that should threaten anybody. Why shouldn't we permit a quiet suicide when the quality of life is no longer there?

A: What a seductive argument that is, especially when we know of older people who are suffering through a slow, painful death. It does seem more humane to allow them to go to sleep quietly and escape all their misery. It is my firm conviction, however, that untold sorrow for millions of people lies down that road.

The problem, aside from the moral issues of taking human life, is that euthanasia is inevitably *progressive* in nature. Once you let that snake out of the basket, it will be impossible to control where it slithers! Let me illustrate.

Suppose we legalize physician-assisted suicide for elderly people who are terminally ill. The question is, how would it be limited thereafter for those who were neither sick nor severely handicapped? How about an older but healthy man who was simply tired of living? Could we really require a note from his physician in order to permit his suicide?

Then if the old but healthy can choose to die, what about the not-so-old? Could a 50 year-old person take the plunge? If not, why not? How about a 40 year-old woman in menopause or a man in mid-life crisis? When you stop to think about it, age has nothing to do with the decision. A 20 year-old depressed homemaker would be as entitled to "death with dignity" as the terminally ill.

If euthanasia is legal for anyone, you see, it will soon become legal for everyone. Neither age, health factors nor quality of life could be defended as qualifiers. The Hemlock Society, which actively promotes euthanasia, certainly understands that fact. They speak confidently about a "right to die" . . . for every human being.

Let's extend that concept now to its worst-case scenario, as suggested by anti-euthanasia activist, Rita Marker. Suppose Diane is an 18 year-old high school senior who is loved greatly by her family. One day, she fails to come home from school when expected. By six-thirty that evening, her mother is starting to worry. When eight o'clock rolls around, her father calls the police. There's been no report of an accident, he is told. None of the local hospitals has a patient named Diane. Mom then begins making frantic telephone calls and finally reaches Diane's best friend, Rene. "Oh, Mrs. Johnson," Rene says with compassion. She begins to cry. "I wanted so much to call you, but I promised Diane I would let the clinic tell you."

"Clinic? What clinic!" asks Mrs. Johnson.

"You know," says Rene. "The Life Clinic downtown. I think you'd better call them."

Diane's mother gets the clinic administrator on the line, who says, "I'm terribly sorry, Mrs. Johnson, we were just getting ready to call you. I know this will be hard for you, but please sit down. Diane came in this afternoon and asked to be assisted in her passing. You may know that she had been very depressed about her grades and because of the rejection letter she received from the college of her choice. Then when her boyfriend let her down . . . well, she just didn't want to go on living. And as you know, 'right to die' laws now apply to every adult 18 years old and over.

"I know this is difficult for you, but it's what Diane most wanted. It was her choice and she is entitled to control her own body. I assure you she was very peaceful as she left us, and her last words were an expression of love for her family."

Does that story seem too far-fetched to be credible? Perhaps. But who would have thought in 1950 that we would soon be filling garbage bags with perfectly formed premature babies who were mangled or burned to death with salt? Could we have imagined that 25 million of these precious children would be torn from their mothers' wombs?

Can anyone believe that we are incapable of killing *any* population of people—especially those who want to die—when we have wreaked such violence on the most defenseless in our midst?

Historically, those nations which have opened the door to the monster of euthanasia have slid into a nightmare of murder. This is precisely what happened in Nazi Germany. They began by killing the sick and old; then they destroyed the mentally ill, mentally retarded, and infants born with deformities. From there, it was but a small step to begin exterminating "undesirables"—the Jews, Poles, Gypsies, the non-productive, political prisoners, and others. Euthanasia was the first small step down the road toward the extermination camps.

Even if this epidemic of murder did not occur, it is certain that "right to death" laws would result in a dramatic increase in the number of suicides occurring annually. Each death would represent incalculable grief, guilt, and sorrow for those left behind.

Suicide may look like an easy way out for the one who dies, but it is perhaps the most painful experience in living for loved ones and relatives—many of whom would certainly be children. We draw the same conclusion from every angle: the curse of euthanasia must *never* be released upon our people!

Q: What do you predict regarding the future? Will "right to die" laws be passed?

A: I fear that they will, first because the media has taken euthanasia as one of its cherished causes. Once the power of the press is focused on a specific issue of this nature, it's only a matter of time until the people begin to change their views. That is especially true today when our public policy decisions are made by opinion polls rather than deeply held moral and ethical convictions.

But there is another reason legalized suicide is likely to plague us, according to our former Surgeon General, Dr. C. Everett Koop. Dr. Koop once told me the euthanasia movement will someday dwarf the abortion phenomenon because of what he called "the squaring of the pyramid."

Through the centuries, age patterns of populations have been triangular in nature. The greatest number of people in a society were the youngest, represented by the base of the pyramid. The fewest number were the oldest, symbolized by the peak. In our society, however, these classic demographics have been modified. The huge number of babies born after World War II are now passing through mid-life and will soon square off the top of the pyramid.

Conversely, the effect of abortion on demand has thinned the ranks of the young. These unusual patterns will create enormous problems for us in a few years. As the large number of baby-boomers moves into their fifties, sixties and seventies, we will experience a serious crisis in the provision of health care. There will be fewer younger workers to support this cloud of retiring folks, saddling the newer generation with a heavy financial burden.

Dr. Koop offered this example. He said, consider the pressure that will accumulate on a 40 year-old man who has a 20 year-old daughter in college and a 60 year-old mother with cancer. Since health insurance will be too expensive to afford, the man will be responsible for all his mother's medical bills.

If the mother goes through chemotherapy and several surgeries during the progression of her disease, he will lose his house and his daughter will have to drop out of school. This fact has not escaped his mother's attention. She feels like a burden to her family anyway, but now her condition threatens to bankrupt the family.

But wait! There is a solution. If she will do the honorable thing and check out a little early, she can protect the well-being of those she loves. In this way, the pressure on many in the older generation to accept physician-assisted suicide will be irresistible.

You may remember that former Governor of Colorado, Richard D. Lamm, endorsed this notion. He argued that it is the responsibility of the elderly to get out of the way. Nice guy, Governor Lamm.

The elderly in Holland know full well what euthanasia means to them. Twenty-five percent of all deaths in that country are physician-assisted suicides. An elderly patient in a Dutch nursing home does not know whether the doctor has come to treat him or turn out the lights. What a wicked system!

Q: You spoke of a conspiracy to capture the hearts and minds of children by those who seek to reorder society's dominant values. Who needs a conspiracy when

**mothers and fathers are already so eager to let out-
siders take charge of their children?**

A: I agree, in a sense. The pace of living has become so
frantic that we don't have time for our kids. That situation makes us willing to accept surrogate parenting un-
critically from the "experts" who meander through our
lives. Some parents resist the cultural mindset, but the
pressure to get out of the way and let various authorities
take over for them can be quite severe.

I'm reminded of a mother who told me that she took
her 14 year-old daughter to their pediatrician for a rou-
tine physical exam. The mother was aware that her
daughter was beginning to develop physically and might
be sensitive to her being in the examining room with
her. She offered to remain in the waiting room, but the
girl objected.

"I don't want to go in there by myself," she said.
"Please come with me." After arguing with her daughter
for a moment, the mother agreed to accompany her to
the examining room.

When the exam was over, however, the doctor
turned to the mother and criticized her for intruding. He
said in front of the girl, "You know, you really had no
business being in the examining room. It is time I related
directly to your daughter. You should not even be aware
of the care that I give her or the medication I prescribe.
You shouldn't even know the things that are said
between us. My care of your daughter should now be a
private matter between her and me."

The girl had been going through a period of rebel-
lion, and the mother felt her authority was weakened
by the doctor's comments. It was as though he were
saying, "Your day of supervision of your daughter has
now passed. She should now make her own decisions."

Fortunately, that mother was unwilling to do as she was told, and promptly found a new doctor. Good for her!

I have discussed this conversation with several pediatricians, and they have each agreed with the doctor in this case. They emphasized the importance of a youngster having someone to talk with in private. Perhaps. But I disagree with the autonomy demanded by the physician.

Fourteen year old boys and girls are not grown, and their parents are still the best people to care for them and oversee their development. It is appropriate for a physician to have some private moments with his young patient, but he should never forget to whom he is accountable!

Furthermore, if greater authority is to be granted to the doctor, the parent had better find out just what he believes about contraceptives for minors, premarital sex, spiritual matters, and the like. Be careful whom you choose to trust with the body—and the soul—of your child. Educators, youth ministers, athletic coaches, music instructors, psychologists, counselors, and physicians are there to *assist* parents in raising their kids, not to replace them.

Q: **Recent legislation clearly favors women who are employed outside the home. For example, working women are able to shield their income in IRAs while full-time homemakers cannot. Likewise, the child care bill passed by the Senate in 1989 would tax single income, stay-at-home moms more in order to provide a service for two income families with employed mothers. That is unfair and everyone knows it. Why would Congress discriminate against full time homemakers in this way?**

A: I think the answer is rather simple. Money makes congressional wheels turn. In this day of staggering taxation, however, the people have already been bled white by big spenders in Washington. How, government wonders, can they extract more bucks from the pockets of the common man and woman? By encouraging the second member of a family to seek formal employment. Not only is the working woman's additional salary taxable, but the cumulative income places *both* workers in a higher tax category. In other words, the second income causes the first salary to be taxed more heavily. The result? More dollars are generated for Congress to confiscate and squander on their pet projects.

Q: **Do you really believe Congress is conscious of their bias against homemakers?**

A: I certainly do. We've spent eleven years attempting to get fair and equitable treatment for homemakers, but it has been an uphill fight. The resistance from some Congressmen has been remarkable.

Another thing we're dealing with is the difference in lobbying pressure on this issue. Homemakers have almost *no* voice in Washington, except for that of Focus on the Family, The Family Research Council, Eagle Forum, and Concerned Women for America. On the other side, however, are the formidable resources of the feminists, the abortionists, NOW, the unions, the National Education Association, university women's associations, and dozens of other powerful lobbying groups.

Congressmen would much rather please the vocal women who camp in their waiting rooms than appeal to some theoretical constituency back in their districts. Besides, everyone knows homemakers are thinking about something else.

Q: You obviously would like to see homemakers become better organized.

A: To be sure! Women generally are the key to cleaning up the mess we are facing in this family-unfriendly nation! If we ever get conservative women concerned enough to stand up for what they believe, we could reverse much of the damage done in this half-century. If they would simply ban together to vote a few liberal senators and congressmen out of office—just one time—word would spread like wildfire on the Hill. Henceforth, when the New Traditionalist Women showed up in their outer offices, the yawns and snickers would vanish. Oh, how I wish! We have the numbers! But who will forge them into one mighty voice?

Q: You mentioned some areas of activism in which people should get involved to save the family. I'm sure you didn't intend for that list to be complete or final. Would you give us some additional ideas for using our influence in the best manner?

A: I could list hundreds of possibilities, if pressed to do so. What follows are the areas where the need for citizen participation is acute. *Thank you* for requesting this information.

1. Work to help the homeless in your community—especially where children are involved.
2. Form a community action group to fight pornography—or participate in an existing group.
3. Raise money at bake sales to donate pro-family books to your local library.
4. Take advantage of the opportunities that may be available in your local public school district to review textbooks that are being considered for

adoption. Let the school board know of any anti-religious or immoral biases in the books.

5. Register to vote and encourage others to do the same.
6. Join the citizen's committee that governs cable TV in your community.
7. Volunteer your time with an AIDS support group, thus providing a Christian response to this dreaded disease.
8. Teach a Sunday school class on social-action issues affecting Christians.
9. Find out if your local phone company offers dial-a-porn services, and if so, start a campaign against it.
10. Monitor local judges and their decisions, keeping in mind that many of these jurists face reelection contests. Be sure to hold them accountable.
11. Start a social-action committee at your church.
12. Join your political party's local precinct committee.
13. Join a local pro-life group, or a state coalition.

These and many other worthy causes need people like you and me to take part, to lend moral and financial support, and to take up the banner for restoring decency and moral values in every corner of this nation. I challenge every one of you to let your voice be heard.

_____ *A Word of Introduction* _____

It is now my privilege to introduce my good friend, Gary Bauer, who will add his perspective on the second great civil war which engulfs us. Gary is certainly well qualified for the task. As the former Under Secretary, Department of Education, and later as Senior Domestic Policy Advisor to President Reagan, he has worked to defend the institution of the family at the highest levels of government.

I met Gary more than ten years ago at a White House meeting that brought us together. We developed an immediate friendship as we realized how many values and beliefs we held in common. My admiration grew steadily as I watched him function within the Reagan Administration, especially during the latter years when he was one of the last remaining conservatives on the senior White House staff.

Gary faced unrelenting pressure for his courageous defense of traditional values, but he never flinched. He held lightly the privileges of his position—the beautiful oak-paneled office near the President and the chauffeur-driven limousine which delivered him to important meetings around town. He put it all on the line every day. Believe me, it is unusual to find a member of that secular Washington scene who believes passionately in the family and is willing to risk his own comforts to defend it!

Toward the end of President Reagan's second term, Gary resigned his post and prepared for the next phase of his professional life. As an attorney with high government experience, he received many generous offers. A law firm in D.C. invited him to join their partnership at a salary that surprised even Gary. Characteristically, he declined and accepted instead a position with our organization at about half the salary. Why? Because he is convinced that the institution of the family is in grave danger and he wants to help defend and preserve it.

Gary Bauer now serves as President of the Family Research Council, the Washington office of Focus on the Family. As such, he and a staff of fifteen work tirelessly in a city where families have very few supporters.

Gary grants about twenty interviews with the press and media every day, articulating the values for which we stand. Gary also continues to consult with the White House and the Congress on family-related issues. He is, I believe, one of America's great resources in this day of national peril.

I will join you again for a few concluding comments in the final chapter.

Gary L. Bauer

5

WASHINGTON
AND THE FAMILY

The sound started as a low rumble deep in his stomach. It slowly began to build in intensity. Finally, a burp emerged from our son Zachary that would qualify for a place in the *Guinness Book of World Records*, in the "burps by two year-olds" category.

Every parent worries that his child will do something like this—perhaps in front of a neighbor or a prim and proper aunt. Mine chose to show his stuff in the presence of the President of the United States.

The occasion was my last day at the White House after serving President Reagan in a variety of positions for eight years. My wife and I, and our very excited children, had a few intimate minutes in the Oval Office with the President to say goodbye. Then we walked a few yards away to the ornate Roosevelt Room where a hundred close friends and colleagues gathered to wish me good luck.

The President, as is customary when a presidential assistant leaves, was saying a few kind words about me. Just about the time he started praising my work, our son broke the magic of the moment with his gastric surprise.

Fortunately, my wife was holding him near the President's "bad" ear so I'm not sure if the Commander-In-Chief heard the sonic boom. But he must have wondered why my 100 friends broke into laughter at the very moment he was praising my good work. Oh well, Zach will have a great story to tell his children.

In retrospect, the incident seems a fitting end to my service in government. During those eight years I had argued for, and promoted, the American family. I had pled the case for millions of mothers who endure runny noses, dirty diapers, spilled drinks and untimely burps, out of love and a commitment to nurturing and civilizing a new generation.

At policy tables where conversation often turned to arcane economic theories and the latest editorial in the *Washington Post*, I had often caused embarrassed silences by speaking about the simple virtues of these mothers who deserved our help and praise. My son's burp and the smile that followed it was a little reminder in the corridors of power that life is more than budget numbers and congressional hearings.

During my years in Washington the most surprising and profoundly disappointing thing I discovered was just how little appreciation there is for the nurturing things that are done by the common people who keep America running.

In the halls of government whenever we were discussing the importance of religious faith, or the sacrifices of stay-at-home mothers, or the exploitation of women and children by pornography, there was an unease or even an embarrassment about such issues. "Why is this fellow bringing up those things when we have to deal with the latest round of trade negotiations or decide on the proper disbursement of impact aid funds?"

Washington is a "green eye shade" city where number crunchers are in high demand. What is rare is the public policy professional willing to deal with the real problems faced by real families. What is even rarer are public officials who believe in the moral, social, and family traditions that are at the core of American life, and that are under attack from every corner.

In the rarefied atmosphere of Washington, traditional family values seem alien or not sufficiently important to affect policy substantially. Even worse, many politicians hire speech writers to help them put together pro-family rhetoric to embellish their oratory. All too often the pro-family commitment doesn't go beyond words. Instead, words are merely tools used to gain power and keep it.

Inside the Administration

I have no doubt that Ronald Reagan felt that America must rededicate itself to the family. But even during his Administration, family issues sometimes received little attention at the staff level. An early sign of how some officials felt about these issues became apparent in the first few days of the new Administration.

January of 1981 was an incredible time. I showed up at the ornate Old Executive Office Building right next to the White House. There, hundreds of support staff were busy at work getting the new Administration off to a fast start.

My heart was racing. After months in the campaign this was the prize. I was actually part of the White House staff. Of course, my position was far down the chain of command. In fact, Martin Anderson, the head of the Office of Policy Development, was not quite sure where or how to assign me.

I tried to make myself useful any way I could during those first few weeks, including going out and picking up other staff members' lunches. Even though I had a law degree from prestigious Georgetown University, I felt no loss of pride in doing mundane tasks. I was just happy to be in this building where great men had made momentous decisions that altered the course of American history.

It was in this atmosphere that a key strategy meeting took place to determine which issues would receive the most attention. We were seated at a large table in what had been the office of the Secretary of War before World War II. I don't mind admitting I was intimidated by some of my colleagues.

Seated at the table were a dozen top notch intellectuals whose job it was to develop presidential policy. As we went around the table, each expert made the case for the issues they thought should be emphasized. Not surprisingly, the environmentalist argued for the environment, the economist for the economy, the housing expert for housing reform and on down the line. Finally my turn came.

"Why hasn't anyone mentioned the family issues?" I said. "Those issues caused more Democrats to vote for the President than any other factor. We need to talk about values, school prayer, lower taxes for families, right to life, and educational choice!"

There was a moment of hesitation and then the head of the Office, Martin Anderson, said, "Fine, Bauer—those issues are yours."

I was astonished! The most important topics in the campaign were being delegated to the lowest fellow on the totem pole—me! Obviously, some of those present were hoping that the issues would go away. It was an early lesson that if the family was going to be protected, I would have to fight for it, even in a conservative Administration.

Six years later, I had worked my way into a senior advisory position to deal with those same pro-family issues, but it was still a struggle to achieve a fair shake for them. Washington just hasn't been geared to think of the family!

The average politician is extremely lucky that American citizens are too busy with lawn mowers, braces, and mortgage payments to take a hard look at what is happening in the corridors of power. It is my hope they will get angry enough to inform themselves some day.

I predict that when they do, there will be a "house cleaning" that will not only send a lot of elected officials into early retirement, but will also prove once and for all that the only special interest group that really matters in this country is the average American family.

Washington Is Different

It is hard for an "outsider" to imagine just how culturally, economically, and politically isolated Washington, D.C. —"The Puzzle Palace on the Potomac"—is from the rest of the country.

The economic statistics alone tell an interesting story. According to *Sales and Marketing Management*'s 1989 survey of buying power, the D.C. region has the highest average family income after taxes of any area in the country: $48,613. That is more than $15,000 higher than the national average. The three richest jurisdictions in America all happen to be Northern Virginia suburbs—the homes of Washington bureaucrats and lobbyists.

In spite of all this wealth, Washington has no major industry nor is it known for any product. Its citizens are wealthy because it is the home of government—a government that produces laws, speeches, and regulations while it pays itself handsomely with the tax money of America's families.

But economics don't tell the whole story. Washington is different in other ways too. The average Washingtonian is much less likely than the rest of America to sew, read the Bible, or play with the grandchildren.

The most common activities, according to a survey by *National Demographics and Lifestyles,* include attending the theater, watching the Sunday public affairs shows, dabbling in real estate, and engaging in "career oriented activities." These activities aren't necessarily bad, but few American families have the resources or time to do them after raising kids and paying bills.

Of course the problem is much deeper. Washington is a city where "liberalism" is in the saddle. The *Washington Post* dictates the policy direction, even when a conservative President sits in the Oval Office. The city government itself has been in the hands of far-out liberals for years. And the small town that exists inside the Washington metropolitan beltway—the 30,000 lobbyists, Congressional aides, top-level bureaucrats, political activists and camp followers—are immersed in and promote an anti-traditional culture.

Even pro-family members of Congress can become disoriented in this atmosphere. Traditional families are nowhere to be seen. It is easy to accept the line that the traditional family is dead, particularly when all the women on your staff are single, or have children in child care, or support abortion rights.

Washington responds to the special interests. Interspersed between the historical monuments is another type of monument—the multi-million dollar buildings owned by the mega-lobbyists speaking for labor, business, education groups, and hundreds of alphabet-soup names that most Americans would only vaguely recognize, if at all.

From the Fertilizer Institute to the Association of Associations, Washington is a town that responds to political pressure. These groups hire thousands of smooth talking lobbyists adept at speaking the lingo of "inside the beltway" talk. Members of Congress, bureaucrats, reporters—the movers and shakers—are all accustomed to asking the questions, "What does big labor want? What will the business community say?" The question that is seldom asked is, "What does the average family want and need?"

You only have to be here a very short time to understand the wisdom of the founding fathers. They wanted and assumed members of Congress would be "citizen politicians" who would spend most of their time living and working in the communities they are supposed to represent.

But contrary to that vision, Washington is controlled by an entrenched establishment firmly in the grip of an anti-family and anti-traditional-values philosophy. Politicians make weekend trips home, but they seldom connect with the real concerns of the hard-working Americans who are over-taxed and over-regulated.

The Power Crowd

Washington is filled with people obsessed with getting power, keeping it, and using it. The price that is paid is usually principle. And since Washington is profoundly liberal—from the media to its cultural elites—the pressure to abandon principle is particularly strong on those who come here as advocates of traditional values.

What a tragedy! Power is a passing thing. No one holds it for long. Don Regan was one of the most powerful Chiefs of Staff that ever resided in the White House. He conducted activities with an iron fist. When I was called to his office to defend or explain an action, it was time for high anxiety. Yet in one day all that power evaporated. Don Regan learned of his dismissal by hearing it on the television set in his office.

The next day, as I entered the West Wing of the White House to meet the new Chief of Staff, Howard Baker, I ran into Don Regan. He was carrying a box filled with his personal possessions out of the building. Suddenly the aura of authority was gone. A man who once bragged that nothing happened in the White House without his knowledge was, in 24 hours, reduced to just another fellow cleaning out his office to make room for the next guy.

The American family and our children desperately need politicians whose first priority is not their own aggrandizement. We need public servants who won't bend just because of what the editorial board of the *Washington Post* has just written. We need men and women unashamed to stand for the permanent values and beliefs that common men and women hold dear.

A Case Study

I learned just how ignorant of the family Washington politicians are when I was assigned to prepare a major report on the family in January of 1986.

President Reagan, acting through the Attorney General, gave me 120 days to report to the White House on problems facing the American family. The assignment was broad. I was asked to review its critical role in perpetuating civilization, examine the breakdown of the family and the social disorder it has produced, and to evaluate what role government had played in this breakdown. Finally, I was to recommend to the President steps we could take to help support families now.

Interestingly, the idea of such a review originated with my co-author, Dr. James Dobson. During a White House briefing in January 1984, Jim had made a series of suggestions about the family to President Reagan, including a complete examination of government programs and their impact on the home. That the report was ultimately done is evidence of the impact one citizen can have!

The last time the White House had become involved this directly in family policy was a disastrous 1980 White House "Conference on Families" staffed by the Carter Administration. For many Americans, that Conference represented everything that was wrong in the last 20 years in

Washington's handling of family issues. In fact, the befuddled delegates, many of them left-wing activists, couldn't even agree on what a family was. Needless to say, it's tough to advocate public policy if you can't even define the subject under discussion.

The report I was asked to write represented a chance, from a traditional perspective, to bring the plight of the family to national attention and to show how its health was crucial to the future of the country.

In the weeks that followed, a team of a dozen government experts was assembled from various Cabinet Departments and Agencies. Each was assigned the job of reviewing regulations in their agency that might be hurting families and undermining the rights and responsibilities of parents.

Advice was solicited from hundreds of outside experts representing a cross section of the political spectrum, from the NAACP to the conservative Heritage Foundation. Each organization was asked what one thing they would do to make government more "family friendly."

As the information poured in, our working group spent long hours in the evening, after their normal daytime jobs were finished, to examine the material and formulate recommendations. Finally, after months of study, the time came to write our report.

The Washington bureaucracy has the ability to take the most passionate issues and turn them into bureaucratic pap. I was determined that was not going to happen with this report. I was intent on making sure that it would not sound lifeless and passionless like so many other government documents. I decided to write the document myself, and I asked my colleagues to review it as we went along.

After dozens of meetings, and then a final presentation to the White House Domestic Policy Council, I was given the green light by the Administration to introduce the report to the public. I knew, of course, that some of the recommendations would generate public debate, but even so, I was not prepared for the firestorm that was about to erupt.

Fire on the Hill

As I entered the press room to present the report, entitled *The Family: Preserving America's Future*, it was apparent that we had the attention of the media. At the podium was a bank of microphones—dozens of them. At the back of the room were cameras from the major TV networks. The room was filled with representatives of Washington's myriad lobbying and special interest groups, as well as dozens of reporters from major newspapers.

Advance copies of the report had been supplied to the press as a matter of courtesy. Everyone in the room had read it, and from the grimaces on most of their faces, it was clear that they didn't like what they saw.

I began my presentation by joking that my interest in the family was more than theoretical; my wife Carol was due to deliver our third child any moment. No one cracked a smile. These folks were ready for combat. After a brief presentation and silent prayer for wisdom and strength, I opened the press conference for questions.

The questions came like gunfire. Almost universally, they were negative and argumentative. There was no hint of objectivity. This wasn't a press conference, it was a roast, and I was to be their dinner.

Some of the questions zeroed in on specific policy recommendations, but most dwelled on my rhetoric. One paragraph, in particular, seemed to send the establishment into philosophical seizures. It was a simple statement in which I expressed a basic tenet of American life.

> It is time to reaffirm some "home truths" and to restate the obvious. Intact families are good. Families who choose to have children are making a desirable decision. Mothers and

fathers who then decide to spend a good deal of time raising those children themselves, rather than leaving it to others, are demonstrably doing a good thing for those children. Countless Americans do these things every day. They ask for no special favors—they do these things naturally out of love, loyalty and a commitment to the future. They are the bedrock of our society. Public policy and the culture in general must support and reaffirm these decisions —not undermine and be hostile to them or send a message that we are neutral.

This celebration of the norm, this verbal praise of family values and the assertion that private choices had public consequences, was just too much for Washington's liberal press corps to handle. The accepted wisdom in this city holds the exact opposite of what I had stated in the report.

When I called certain choices good and desirable I was, by implication, calling other choices bad and undesirable. This is the ultimate "sin" in Washington. I was making value judgments in a culture that talks in non-judgmental terms about "lifestyles," not about commitment or fidelity.

The next morning I found myself in one of those Washington firestorms that cause so many political appointees to hide under their desks. Then they run back home in a couple of years, confident that if no one noticed them or criticized them they must have done a good job. Their highest ideal is to be unnoticed and, therefore, not criticized or ridiculed. They tell the voting population in their districts what a terrific job they have done. Clearly I had violated that policy.

Facing the Music

The articulate, liberal Senator from New York, Daniel Patrick Moynihan, called my report "less a policy paper than a tantrum." My "friends" in the White House suddenly seemed nervous. Rumors spread that I would resign. One social scientist was quoted in the press as saying that my interpretation of family trends did "just what the Reagan Administration says government should not do—set the values for how people should live their lives."

Of course the Reagan Administration had never said any such thing. All institutions, from government to the schools, have an obligation to hold up values and urge citizens to live good and decent lives.

But other parts of the report came under fire as well. We recommended that government must restore the authority of the family and of parents. Much to the chagrin of the bureaucratic busy bodies in the nation's Capital, we asserted that when intervention in family life was necessary, "it should be undertaken by institutions closest to control by citizens . . . churches, neighborhood groups and voluntary organizations."

There was nothing in this report to provide an opportunity for new Washington bureaucracies to be set up to help solve problems that government had caused in the first place.

The welfare lobby was also outraged. They fired their rhetorical guns at one recommendation in particular. Our report said,

> Government should not provide incentives—or make things easier—for teenagers tempted to promiscuity. Specifically, single mothers under the age of 21 should not be given subsidized housing apart from their own parents. AFDC (Aid to Families with Dependent Children) should be restructured in a similar way. These steps would go a long way toward making illegitimate motherhood less attractive in the poverty culture.

This seemed like common sense to me. Government should reward good behavior and discourage bad behavior. But Washington is a city addicted to giving away taxpayers' money to everyone. That way, they build power bases for themselves and secure employment and influence into the ensuing years.

For the welfare community, my recommendation threatened their base of power. To suggest a linkage between assistance and behavior was heresy. The large, well-paid welfare establishment that claims to speak for the poor quickly accused us of being heartless. But, in fact, the policy we recommended would make it less attractive for a young woman to conceive a second child out of wedlock, and would improve her chances of escaping poverty. Research clearly shows that a teenager who has an out-of-wedlock child is unlikely to have a second one *if* she continues to live with her parents.

Rounding out the list of recommendations was a call to do away with value-free sex education classes in the schools, an end to the distribution of birth control devices to minors without parental permission, tax relief for families instead of special interest groups, better policies to encourage adoption, and the appointment of federal judges who respected family and traditional values. In short, our report managed to fly in the face of the conventional wisdom on nearly every major issue. Predictably, the other side struck back with an intense media barrage.

Tackling the Controversy

I was in no mood to back down in the face of the criticism. In the days that followed I went on every radio and TV talk show I could. I visited the editorial boards of major newspapers and aggressively argued the pro-family case. I learned a long time ago that being "controversial" in Washington meant you had the unsettling habit of speaking the truth in plain words.

I decided that if this issue would eventually drive me out of my appointive office, I could live with that fact. But I wouldn't have been able to face my own family if I backed down under fire. I believed what I had written. I believe it still. This is where I resolved to stand.

In the days that followed the tide began to turn. *USA Today*, generally liberal in its editorial views, endorsed the report, saying,

> Strong families are the cornerstone of the USA. They play a vital role in our free society. Federal policies should not ignore or penalize families. Intact families are good. That's the message of a new Reagan Administration report called *The Family: Preserving America's Future*. It's a simple message, but it's one we need to hear.[1]

In side by side columns by Senator Moynihan and myself, even he reluctantly conceded that some of the recommendations were worth serious study. Others came to my defense. *The Detroit News* editorialized,

> Actually [the report] is exactly the reverse of a tantrum. It is a rational statement of common sense approaches toward the most vexing, intricate, and intimate social problems faced by our culture.[2]

More importantly, requests for the report started pouring in from just plain folks from all over the country, and thousands were distributed. To me, the requests were a personal vindication and thousands were distributed.

A year later when I was sworn in at the White House as President Reagan's Domestic Policy Advisor, we were still reprinting the report to meet the persistent demand for it.

Unfortunately, most of our recommendations required Congressional action—by a Congress whose liberal Committee Chairmen were basically hostile to the values represented by our report. I didn't expect quick implementation, and the Washington establishment fulfilled my lowest expectations.

It didn't matter that most public opinion polls showed that the American public overwhelmingly supported most of our recommendations. The troika of powerful Washington bureaucrats, media, and lobbyists dug in their heels and waited until the recommendations faded from public memory.

During those tedious months I experienced firsthand the deep and probably unbridgeable split between America's liberal establishment and those countless millions of Americans for whom family and faith are the pillars of their lives.

Government Must Be Family Friendly

As the twentieth century marches to a close, it will be remembered for many things by future generations. Perhaps the most loathsome historical fact will be that our century witnessed the creation of the most bloodthirsty totalitarian governments in world history.

These all-powerful governments, from Communism to Nazism, and from Idi Amin in Uganda to Pol Pot in Cambodia, tolerated no private area of life. As Mussolini put it, "Everything for the state. Nothing against the state. Nothing outside the state."

History is replete with despots, but few can rival the totalitarian leaders, from Stalin to Hitler, who sought to fold every aspect of life into the government sphere and who treated men and women as mere pieces of dust to be crushed and reformed in their own images.

It is not surprising that every totalitarian movement of the twentieth century has not only tried to destroy the individual but also to destroy the family—to make it a mere bureau of government. All modern totalitarian movements have tried to substitute the power of the state for the rights, responsibilities, and authority of the family. Strong families can stand against the aggression of government and protect the individual, but not without struggle.

When all power flows to government, with no mediating institutions between government and the individual, the result has been disaster and tragedy. In fact, in this century of bloody wars, totalitarian governments have killed more of their own people for political reasons than all the soldiers killed in all the wars of this century combined.

Often the first area of conflict between the family and gargantuan government has been over the control of children. In the United States we have seen the tendency to let government assume more responsibility for, and power over, children, even while parental rights and authority have eroded. If this trend continues, I am convinced it will be our greatest mistake as a nation!

Adolph Hitler understood instinctively how important it would be for the "Thousand Year Reich" to control the children. He said, "When an opponent declares, 'I will not come over to your side,' I calmly say, 'Your child belongs to us already . . . what are you? You will pass on. Your descendants, however, now stand in the new camp. In a short time they will know nothing else but this new community.'"

It is against such abuse of power that our founding fathers set up our democratic system of government with its checks and balances. They believed strongly that each individual has natural God given rights, and that no government can take them away. A moral people with strong faith, and a nation living in strong families, were seen as the natural protection against unchecked government and the growth of tyranny.

Even in "free countries," there has been a tendency in this century for governmental power to expand and grow at the expense of the family. Well-intentioned welfare programs have made government a substitute husband and father to millions of inner city women and children. While these programs may have been designed for compassionate reasons, it is doubtful we will ever see human renewal in our urban inner cities without the retreat of government and the re-establishment of Black men in positions of responsibility within their own families and communities.

Government's Greed

The erosion of family autonomy and authority has occurred in "slow motion" in the United States, but the trend is clear. From year to year, less turf is left to the family and more power is taken by, or given to, government. One looks at government's ever growing tentacles and is reminded of the story told by Lincoln about an aggressive farmer. "I'm not greedy about land," said the farmer, "I only want what joins mine."

The subjugation of public education to governmental control is a prime example of parental retreat. Until about the mid-nineteenth century, education was a function of the family. Some of its tasks might be delegated to a school-master, or even to a communal school, but control continued to reside in the hands of the family. Today, too many parents instinctively think of education as a matter entirely for the government-run schools. Those who reserve the authority over their children's education for themselves are thought by many to be "strange." Parents who home-school their kids get funny looks from their friends. Perhaps, a century from now, the same funny looks will go to parents who feed, clothe, and house their children at home instead of consigning them to government child-factories.

This trend toward delegation of family functioning must be reversed, and there is no time to lose. Politicians need to hear from their constituents in language that is crystal clear.

Few of the advocates of government control openly describe their proposals as anti-family. In fact, many of them propose their new legislation and regulations while mouthing pro-family rhetoric. We are even willing to concede that many of them actually believe they are helping the family.

All too often, however, their proposals have hastened the destruction of the family unit and the transfer of authority from parents to government. As citizens we must make sure that our elected officials are not only mouthing the right words but also are singing them to the right tune.

Most importantly, government policy on the family should follow the Hippocratic oath: "First of all, do no harm." The family cannot withstand many more blows from "unintended consequences." If government officials cannot clearly demonstrate how their proposals will help the family and return authority, rights, and resources to it, then their ignorance should be reason enough to take no action on the plans they propose.

We do believe there are a number of things that government can and must do to help the family. We outline these in our closing agenda. But our proposals do not require *more* government nor more bureaucracy. They require instead that Uncle Sam give back to the family the resources and authority it needs.

For those who haven't gotten the message already, let me be completely clear. Washington needs a major housecleaning! From the Congress, to the bureaucracy, we need to bring in a new crop of dedicated public *servants* who understand the importance of the family to the future of our society. We need men and women who are willing not only to talk pro-family but to vote that way too. We need public officials with courage and conviction.

A Personal Observation

Let me add a personal comment at this point. At an early age I have been able to experience things in the corridors of power in Washington that few individuals will ever have an opportunity to do. I have walked the historic halls of the White House where portraits of our great presidents hang in a gallery of honor.

I have sat at the Cabinet Table and shared with top government leaders my best advice on the great issues facing our country. I have stood in the Oval Office with the most powerful men in the world, and flown on Air Force One.

On the evening of the State of the Union Address, I traveled by motorcade through the streets of Washington as police parted the traffic for our convenience. Minutes later I sat in the VIP gallery with the White House aides and the First Family to listen to the President outline for the Congress his legislative agenda. I would be lying if I told you these experiences were not important to me. They were.

I will cherish the memories. I have devoted my professional life to the job of influencing public policy. My years in government were a dream come true. But in the quiet moments in my own home, sitting by a fire in my den on a cold wintry day, or lying awake in the early hours of the morning with my wife next to me, it is not these recollections that flood my mind. Rather, it is the special family moments that fill my memory.

I remember the incredible awe I felt in the delivery room when each of our three children was born, the quiet times with my wife when words are not needed, the pride of attending my daughter's honor roll breakfast, or the moment when my children chose to accept the Lord as their Savior and to walk through life with Him.

In a world of siren songs beckoning us to the rocks of destruction—power, lust, money—it is the safe harbor of the family to which we must anchor our lives.

Gary L. Bauer

6

THIRTY YEARS
ON THE
SLIPPERY SLOPE

How did it all happen? When did parents begin to lose control of children to government bureaucrats and an "anything goes" culture? When did "one nation under God" decide it was illegal to even talk about religion and morality in the public arena? When was open season declared on the institution of the family?

Frankly, no one seems certain. No fire alarm rang with a clear signal of danger. No modern day Paul Revere rode through the public square to awaken us from our slumber. Indeed, many of our citizen-soldiers *still* don't know there's a war going on . . . that everything they hold dear is under attack.

It is sometimes difficult to appreciate the effects of gradual but significant change, such as we have seen in this half-century. What we need, it would appear, is a marker of some type—a point of reference that will illustrate how far we have drifted away from traditional values.

That reminds me of a recent trip I took with Carol and our three children to a beautiful dude ranch in Montana. We had gone there for a brief vacation to escape the special madness that is Washington, D.C.

The first morning after breakfast, we saddled up the horses and made preparations for a long ride. Now, I don't mind admitting that I'm uncomfortable around horses, so I told the ranch hands to give me a worn-out nag.

My request was granted. I was hoisted atop a sway-backed beast named Mr. Ed. I soon understood why. Even in his prime, Mr. Ed had never had all four feet off the ground at one time. I kept kicking his sides just to keep him awake.

Wonderful, I thought. *Ed and I are going to spend three exhilarating hours together this morning!*

As the horses slowly lumbered up the mountain, Ed and I fell into last place. It wasn't my idea; he just seemed to want it that way. A wrangler noticed we were losing ground and dropped back to check out the problem. He eyed my steed and me for a moment, and then drawled, "Bauer, pick out a tree and keep your eye on it."

"Sure," I said. "But why?"

"That way you can tell whether or not you're moving."

The wrangler helped me gauge my progress up the mountain; but his suggestion also has particular relevance to the world in which we live. We need a "tree"—a point of reference—that can help us gauge how far America has slid down the slippery slope of moral relativism.

Establishing the Guideposts

Let's take the year 1960 and compare the value system in that day with America's social attitudes three decades later. On the other end, let's designate 1990 as the second marker. What significant changes occurred during that 30 year period?

In 1960, everyone knew that a family meant a husband and wife with or without children. The law defined it a bit more broadly, as people related by blood, marriage, and adoption. Most children were cared for by their parents, and most politicians knew that any effort to strengthen the family was a good idea.

In 1990, politicians can't even agree on what "traditional" families are or whether they are worthy of special assistance. Indeed, a major movement is underway to redefine "family" to mean any group of people which merely *thinks* of itself as family.

A sizable minority of children is supervised by professional caregivers, while some children, called "latchkey" kids, are left with no adult care at all during much of the day. Some opinion leaders point to broken homes, out-of-wedlock pregnancies, and homosexual "couples," not as reasons for alarm, but rather as evidence of healthy family diversity and pluralism.

In 1960, there was a general consensus that religion was a positive influence in American life and that it should be encouraged. Our children routinely began the school day with a simple prayer or moment of silence. It was common at Christmas time to see a nativity scene near city hall. Public service ads on TV urged families to attend church together on Sunday. A billboard read, "The family that prays together, *stays* together."

Today a militant secularism prevails. Any public display of religion, whether a prayer at a high school commencement or a cross on top of a firehouse, is immediately attacked by civil libertarian attorneys.

Recently several government officials in Washington, D.C., called on citizens to join in a day of prayer to ask God to lead the city out of its quagmire of drugs, crime, and suffering. They were immediately attacked by a local

ACLU official who told the *Washington Post,* "It is always inappropriate for government officials to ask citizens to pray."

Lincoln, Jefferson and Roosevelt, among others, would be surprised to hear such an absurd statement, but it is the accepted wisdom today. Our federal courts seem committed to an interpretation of the Constitution that increasingly narrows the ground upon which religious faith is permitted to tread.

In 1960, out-of-wedlock pregnancy was a matter of shame. When it happened, couples often did a quaint thing —they got married, so that the child would have a name and the influence of a father. Girls who "slept around" were often ostracized by their fellow students. A pregnant teenager was sent away to have the child rather than risk the censure of the community.

In 1990, one out of five babies born in America was conceived out of wedlock. In Washington, D.C., illegitimacy was an alarming 55 percent! In many schools, the virtuous girl was considered odd, and was subjected to the same scorn and ridicule once reserved for the "easy" date 30 years earlier. Surveys revealed that many of our sons and daughters were embarrassed to admit their virginity.

In 1960, a divorce was enough to end a politician's career. Most couples stayed together for life. Now more than one million children are affected by divorce every year. Mates are traded in for newer models as if they were cars. For each of the last 15 years, there have been more than one million divorces compared to less than half that many in the early '60s.

In 1960, homosexuality was still "in the closet." It was, as it has been for centuries, "the love that dared not speak its name." The psychiatric profession treated homosexuality as a mental disorder or dysfunction. No politician could survive the disclosure of being homosexual. The notion that special civil rights should be granted to people on the basis of their "sexual orientation" was an absurdity. The word "gay" meant happy.

Today there are few political and social movements as aggressive, powerful, or successful as "gay rights" advocates. Homosexuality is no longer considered a dysfunction but rather an orientation or a "sexual preference." If you oppose homosexuality or condemn it from a moral perspective, you risk being labeled "homophobic"—a "sickness" described as a fear or loathing of homosexuality.

College students who oppose the gay rights agenda on their campuses are expelled for discrimination. Gay politicians celebrate their homosexuality and are routinely reelected. Even a homosexual Congressman who allegedly seduced several male pages was returned to office, and Massachusetts Congressman Barney Frank, who admitted paying for sex with a male prostitute, merely received a slap on the wrist by his fellow Congressmen.

In 1960, students in every American classroom began their day with the Pledge of Allegiance to the flag. History books widely used in the schools explained the religious heritage of the nation and were peppered with stirring illustrations of America's heroes and heroines. Most universities had a solid core curriculum that taught the classics of Western civilization. Students were expected to be familiar with the great writers and philosophers of our culture, as well as our Judeo-Christian heritage.

In 1990, the burning of the American flag was designated by the Supreme Court as a form of free speech, protected by the Constitution. In many American cities, the Pledge of Allegiance was not repeated at all or was suspended after the first few years of school.

Many children were deprived of any serious exposure to American history. When a school did offer history courses, they often presented a "revisionist" viewpoint that emphasized America's sins and failures rather than our forefathers' contributions and triumphs.

University presidents could no longer agree on what every educated American should know. The works of the classical writers and thinkers of our culture had been dropped from many university curricula, being replaced with the rantings of Third World ideologues and revolutionaries. Even great institutions like Stanford University had jettisoned Western civilization as a major focus of their curricula.

These and other tumultuous changes have occurred in the lifetime of many Americans living today. Truly, there were many rugged miles between the "trees" marked 1960 and 1990.

Why Are We Losing?

Again we ask, how did all this happen in such a brief period? How could our traditions, values and concepts of morality have eroded to such a degree? What explains the capitulation of the Judeo-Christian system of thought to secular humanism in the post-war era?

Two points are critical in response to those questions. *First*, let it be understood that the revolutionary social changes we've described did not occur capriciously or accidentally. They were orchestrated rather informally by those who have a specific agenda in mind for the family.

It would be inaccurate to call the social reorientation of American thought and behavior a "conspiracy," *per se*, because it was not centrally coordinated. No high level czars determined society's course in some mysterious smoke-filled room. On the other hand, we are convinced that those who despise the Judeo-Christian system of values—and there are many—worked on a hundred independent fronts to produce a common objective.

As the civil war has grown more heated in recent years, they have labored much more closely to accomplish their goals. Can there be any doubt that the ACLU, National Organization of Women, the National Abortion Rights Action League, People for the American Way, political liberals, and others have joined forces to drive for final victory?

The *second* point is that the victory they seek is not yet in their grasp. The very fact that they have begun to crow about the death of the traditional family is indication that it is alive and kicking. Thus, it has become necessary for them to disseminate misinformation—some call them lies—about the extent of family chaos. This is a point worth explaining in greater detail.

Whatever Happened to Ozzie and Harriet?

In the 1950s, millions of American families gathered around their television sets to watch the Nelson family do their funny thing. Ozzie and Harriet and their two boys, David and Rickie, presented wholesome family entertainment for many years. They were part of a genre of TV shows featuring intact families, including programs like "Father Knows Best," "Leave It to Beaver," "I Love Lucy," and other situation comedies.

These shows usually contained subtle value lessons about honesty, hard work, loyalty, and commitment. Some of the old black and white films from those days are still shown on cable TV networks, proving that there is a continuing appetite for clean, wholesome television programming—even if it is technically flawed and hopelessly out of style.

I doubt if the Nelsons ever thought they would someday become a symbol for traditional values and lifestyles in the '80s and '90s, but that is exactly what has happened.

Curiously, however, it is not the traditionalists who raise the Ozzie and Harriet banner. It is the other side of the cultural divide that uses them—as an object of ridicule and as a symbol of an archaic way of life.

Along with sneering references to "Norman Rockwell's America," the cultural elite frequently remind us that the model of the traditional family—homemaker mother and breadwinner father—is virtually extinct, and they're obviously glad it is gone.

Daniel Seligman, in *Fortune Magazine,* did an analysis of news stories in major papers in 1989. Incredibly, he found 88 instances where Ozzie and Harriet of the '50s were mentioned, and the context was similar in each. As Seligman put it, the usual setting featured a politician "on stage reciting the news that the traditional nuclear family—the kind symbolized by the Nelsons during their marathon stint on black and white TV—was dead or dying."[1]

To add credibility to the claims that the family is dying, a manufactured bit of statistical "evidence" began to appear in liberal jargon. One reporter put it this way:

> It used to be so simple, it seems in retrospect. Dad at the office or factory and mom at home nurturing the next generation. No nightmares that one's child would be abused by someone paid to care. Nor early morning panic when the sitter doesn't show or baby has a fever. No time-consuming search for a center where the prices aren't pegged to the parent's degree of desperation. And no guilt at missing first steps and first words. But the return of those days is about as likely as a prime time comeback of Ozzie and Harriet. *Less than 10 percent of U.S. families are "traditional"—* father at work and mother at home.[2]

The reporter didn't explain her source for the "less than 10 percent" figure, but that number has now become widely accepted as fact. Some writers use even a lower number. John Naisbitt in the best selling book, *Megatrends: Ten New Directions Transforming Our Lives*, puts it this way: " . . . Today, there is no such thing as a typical family. And only a distinct minority (7 percent) of America's population fits the traditional family profile."

Liberal politicians have made good use of this statistical misinformation in recent Congressional debates. Senator Christopher Dodd of Connecticut, one of the leading proponents of federally supported child care, said in March, 1989, "There are [sic] only one in ten American families today where you have a mom at home and dad at work—only one in ten. Ozzie and Harriet are gone."[3]

Congresswoman Pat Schroeder, who can always be counted on to denigrate the family, added her two bits to the child care controversy. She sneered that giving traditional families a role in the child care debate "is like saying the highway program must recognize people who don't drive."[4]

Even conservatives who ran on a pro-family platform got into the act. Senator Orin Hatch cited the 10 percent figure as his reason for supporting child care legislation. It was a very effective argument . . . but a phony one.

It is frustrating to see elected officials, the media, and cultural elites use a deliberate distortion to prove that the traditional family is dead and gone. There is no remorse being expressed in their pronouncements. In fact, their reaction borders on outright glee. But like the rumors of Mark Twain's passing, reports of the demise of the family are greatly exaggerated—often by public officials who should (and do) know better.

Setting the Record Straight

What are the real facts? The Family Research Council went to some lengths to determine the origin of this 10 percent figure, and we found it refers to the families that have an employed father, a stay-at-home mother, and two (count them) *two* children still at home.

What about the family with a go-to-work father, a stay-at-home mother and one child? Sorry, they're not "traditional" according to this contrived definition. What if that mother is a full-time homemaker who is pregnant with her first child? Nope. She and her husband don't qualify.

What about the childless couple which plans for the wife to work for two years so they can buy a home, and then she intends to stay at home and raise a family? You guessed it. They're non-traditional.

Indeed, Jim and Shirley Dobson would be judged "non-traditional" by this definition. Shirley (a former teacher) stayed home and raised their two children for 23 years. She's still there today, but her kids are grown and gone. Sad to say, they're considered non-traditional. Nor do the Bauers make the cut. We have *three* kids being mothered by Carol, a full-time homemaker. We have too many kids! Alas, Ozzie and Harriet couldn't even qualify, now that David is married and Rickie is deceased.

Now let me make clear just how abominable this distortion of truth really is. According to the U.S. Department of Labor, 41.3 percent of all married mothers with preschool children are full-time homemakers. Another 20 percent only work part time, some as few as 10 hours per week in their own homes. That means 61 percent of all mothers who are married with pre-school children are occupied *primarily* in the raising of children.

Furthermore, what does outside employment for the wife have to do with whether or not a family is "traditional" anyway?

Employment is not the key factor. I would define a traditional family as one where husband and wife are lawfully married, are committed to each other for life, and adhere to the traditional values on which the family is based. I can assure you that this model for families is not about to pass from the scene!

Now that the record has been set straight, what can we expect from the propagandists on the left? Well, Pat Schroeder recently sent a promotional letter to her constituency stating . . . just *7.1 percent!* of American families are traditional. So the beat goes on.

Why is this particular statistical distortion so pervasive in public rhetoric today? Because the impact of "cooked statistics" on public policy is significant. As Spencer Rich of the *Washington Post* observed:

> Once in currency, faulty statistics seem to take on a life of their own, gaining momentum from the tendency of the public, once it becomes aware of a trend, to imagine the trend is moving much faster than it really is. For example, a movement away from the traditional family structure is soon interpreted to mean that the traditional family has almost ceased to exist."[5]

Even more dangerous is the risk that loving husbands and wives who read and hear that they represent an insignificant minority will begin to question their decisions to forego extra income and material possessions in order to devote themselves to the raising of children. These are the very people we should be affirming for their sacrificial contributions to the future of our nation. That fact was widely understood until recent years.

To summarize, the game being played is to issue spurious statistics to convince the public that the family has disintegrated, that homemaking is a thing of the past, and that committed husbands and wives have given way to a nation of single parents, unmarried couples, and gay partners. That will permit federal money and the other advantages of national policy to be redirected away from mothers at home.

Now certainly, there are more employed women today than a decade ago, and we're seeing an increasing number of single parent households. Nevertheless, the traditional family has not passed from the scene—nor is it on its deathbed.

The Legal Assault on the Family

The manipulation of statistics is only one method being used by the cultural elite to weaken and immobilize the institution of the family. At a more basic level, they have been working feverishly to revolutionize the understanding of what a family really is.

Political scientists and sociologists began publishing articles in academic journals several years ago, calling for "family diversity." (Whenever you see these words used together, you can be sure the writer is agitating for change.) The shock troops of the movement—the American Civil Liberties Union—then set up the Lambda Legal Defense and Education Fund to promote gay and lesbian rights, including the right of homosexuals to marry.

The repeal of anti-sodomy laws was made a high priority. Then suddenly, in 1988, a series of breakthroughs occurred that have now placed the legal foundation of the family in serious jeopardy.

San Francisco and a half-dozen other California cities passed ordinances allowing unmarried live-in partners, both heterosexual and homosexual, to register their relationships and receive legal recognition as a "domestic partnership." Immediately the ordinances became weapons for the anti-family brigade. The media trumpeted them as a sign of a new era in America. The talk show army shifted into high gear. Earnest commentators took to the airwaves to explain in measured words why any decent American should be happy about this new affirmation of diversity in our country.

Then in July 1989 the Supreme Court of New York dropped a bombshell which not only extended rights to homosexual couples, but also took a gratuitous slap at couples joined in marriage. Two homosexual lovers, Miguel Braschi and Leslie Blanchard, were living in a rent control apartment. When Blanchard, who held the lease, died of AIDS in September of 1986, the landlord asked Braschi to vacate. Braschi refused, claiming that as Blanchard's lover he was "family" and was protected by New York's rent control laws.

Associate Judge Vito J. Titone, writing for a 4 to 2 majority, said that the court could not be influenced by "fictitious legal distinctions" like a marriage certificate or an adoption order to determine what is a family. They ruled that Braschi (who had received a million dollars from the estate of his dead lover) had the right to continue living in the rent control apartment instead of vacating it for a low income family!

It is outrageous that the highest court in the State of New York would consider a marriage license to be irrelevant—a fictitious legal distinction—in defining a family. In an earlier day, Judge Titone and his colleagues would have been impeached. Today, they merely reflect the tenor of the times.

The "change agents" of American culture have their ideological fortresses and they use them to good effect. Once some bizarre social innovation is established in New York or California, the secular media soon promote the idea in the heartland. If legal rights for live-in gay lovers appear outrageous in Kansas or Cincinnati or Peoria today, by tomorrow they will seem more acceptable.

With continual propaganda injected into the culture, the center finally caves in. Good people become afraid or unwilling to stand in front of what appears to be an onrushing train. Tradition yields—the old beliefs recede.

What was once unacceptable and offensive becomes the norm.

Revolutionary Language

The New York court decision was not the first time liberal judges have struck blows against the nuclear family as the basic institution of our society. Writing for the Supreme Court in the *East Cleveland* case, Justice Lewis Powell put the issue this way: "The Constitution prevents (the government) from standardizing its children—and its adults—by forcing all to live in certain narrowly defined family patterns."

When a man and woman with a marriage license and a couple of kids is called by a Supreme Court Justice "a narrowly defined family pattern," Americans should sit up and take notice. *That* is revolutionary! Unfortunately, most citizens will never know about that extraordinary statement.

Not more than one in a thousand ever read that quote or even heard of the East Cleveland case. But in law schools and in gatherings of civil libertarians around the county, such rhetoric is used as a battering ram against one of the last institutions standing in the way of revolutionary social changes—the family.

Shortly after the New York Supreme Court decision, I returned to Washington, D.C., after being out of town on a speaking tour. Carol informed me that the popular television show, "Night Line," had called and wanted me to debate the gay rights issue on TV that evening. Reluctantly, I agreed.

Around midnight I found myself in the studio facing the usual stacked deck. The other guests included a homosexual couple in Madison, Wisconsin, and the president of a group called the Family Diversity Project in Los Angeles. All three, not surprisingly, argued that "family" included anyone and everyone who thought of themselves as a family. The "neutral" moderator made it clear by the nature of his questions that he firmly supported the family diversity people.

Yet even with the odds in their favor, my opponents could not logically defend a position that rejected common sense and basic morality.

I asked whether *three* men joined in a homosexual relationship or one man living with two women should have the same rights as the traditional family? Two of my opponents quickly said "yes." In other words, these informal alliances should have the right to adopt children, file joint tax returns, and qualify for other family benefits. Whether my opponents realized it or not, they had just reopened the polygamy debate.

War always creates casualties, or at least the *risk* of casualties, and the struggle over family, faith and freedom is no exception. Before the evening was over I had received several death threats, merely for defending the basic institution of our culture.

Our office answering machine the next morning contained many recorded messages from self-identified homosexuals using language that was unbelievably vile and obscene. These attacks and threats were in response to my simple argument that a family must be recognized by the law as those related by blood, marriage, or adoption.

But there was also welcome support. An editorial in the *New York Post* entitled "Devaluating Matrimony," seemed to zero in on the implications of the issue. They wrote,

> But if any relationship between people who want these protections and entitlements is sanctified as "marriage," marriage between a man and a woman is deprived of its special and unique status. If two homosexuals can claim the rights of marriage, or two (or more) people who are living together, or a couple of people who happen simply to like each other, "marriage" becomes little more than a

scam to get health benefits and the right to a "spouse's" rent-controlled apartment.[8]

Letters poured into our office over the next several weeks thanking me for the stand I had taken. Some judges and politicians may be confused, but the average American still knows what a family is and apparently stands ready to defend it.

Late that evening after returning home from the ABC studios, I quietly slipped into each of my children's bedrooms to watch them as they slept. My wife, Carol, and I always performed this ritual when our children were very young, just as millions of other parents do. We would tiptoe in, pull up the covers, check for a fevered brow and just reassure ourselves they were alive and well.

But that night I was looking for a different kind of reassurance—one I couldn't find merely with my eyes or ears or touch. I wanted to know that the world my children would grow up in would still embrace and honor the love and commitment between a man and a woman united before God in marriage. I wanted to know that they could have their own children and raise them in a free society that knew the difference between virtue and vice, good and evil, right and wrong.

That night, more than ever, I realized that it wasn't just invisible microbes that threatened the health of my children and the next generations of Americans. Their futures, and our hopes and dreams, were also threatened by an invisible ideology that seemed each day to encroach upon our society, pushing aside the truths that have guided civilized men and women throughout the centuries.

No number of death threats, no amount of media criticism, no amount of pressure would stop me from fighting for these children, or for the millions of others who depend on us to leave them a legacy of freedom and hope.

I believe millions of Americans agree. One of them,

at least, was quoted in an otherwise biased edition of *Newsweek*, devoted to "the changing American family." This unknown gentleman said it best.

"You can call homosexual households 'families' and you can define 'family' any way you want to, but you can't fool Mother Nature. A family is a mommy and a daddy and their children."

I wish I had said that on "Night Line"!

Gary L. Bauer

7

CARING FOR
THE CHILDREN

> It's just a matter of time, it seems, before we have state
> nurseries, which we used to think of as the heartless inven-
> tions of Soviet bureaucrats and Israeli Kibbutzim. Mom
> just can't stay at home. Whether it's inclination or econom-
> ics that sends her out the door every morning doesn't mat-
> ter any more.[1]
>
> Mary McGrory

Few issues more clearly define the two sides of America's cultural civil war than the issue of child care. The
question, "Who cares for the children?" and how we answer
it will determine, to a large extent, what philosophy of living, loving, begetting, and getting through life will prevail
in America in the twenty-first century.

If on this one issue the state wins and our children are
raised from the earliest months by someone other than
their parents, the last and most important function of the
family will have been snatched away. It is possible to lose
other battles over family and children and still live to fight

another day. But losing this one will result, long term, in our losing the war.

In its final report in 1970, The White House Conference on Children made this startling statement. "Day care is a powerful institution. A day care program that ministers to a child from 6 months to 6 years of age has over 8,000 hours to teach him values, fears, beliefs and behaviors."[2]

We agree overwhelmingly! Indeed, that is what concerns us about railroading large numbers of today's preschoolers into government-sponsored child care centers. The temptation to teach this generation a new system of values—one that contradicts the views of their parents—will be almost irresistible. It will place in the hands of the cultural elite—whom we now see as cultural adversaries—all the tools necessary to destroy the Judeo-Christian system of values in a single generation. And it is now within their grasp, at last!

Christopher Lasch critically comments on the vision that some have, in his book, *Haven in a Heartless World*. He writes,

> Parenthood, too important to be left to amateurs and dilettantes, will be professionalized by assigning children to special clinics or, if that seems too cold and impersonal, to couples specially trained and certified for parenthood (a solution advanced by Margaret Mead), or even to communes or other kinds of extended families. The rest of the population, freed from the burdens of child rearing, will find spiritual enrichment in the intensive exploration of one-to-one relationships.[3]

Is this what most Americans want—a world where parents and children only pass each other in the night, and where government decides who cares for the kids? We don't think so, but American society is already moving rapidly in that direction. That austere vision has motivated many of those lobbying for child care legislation for the past two decades.

In 1971, the Congress passed a comprehensive child care bill that Richard Nixon promptly vetoed because, he said, it would "commit the vast moral authority of the national government to the side of communal approaches to child-rearing over the family centered approach."

At the time of his veto, only about 8 percent of America's children were being cared for outside the home in center-based child care. Today, after years of propaganda by the feminists, the media, and the Congress, roughly one in four of our pre-school children are cared for in an organized child care facility.

The Scandinavian Experience

Politicians and media experts cited the experience in Scandinavian countries as models for the United States to follow. In Denmark, for example, only 5 percent of Danish children under the age of six are being raised full time by mothers at home. Twenty-one percent are in some form of private day care and an incredible 55 percent are in public day care.

Fred Hechinger, writing for the *New York Times*, found the Denmark system to be wonderful. He wrote, "If there is a children's paradise look for it in Denmark. You hardly ever hear a child cry."

If you are a parent in Denmark and hardly ever hear a child cry, it is probably because the child is not at home with you but rather in the care of a government bureaucrat.

Seldom mentioned by the experts is the incredible destruction of family life in those nations where government has usurped more and more of the role of the family. For example, one Swedish psychologist said that growing up in Sweden

> . . . involves living with adults, one of whom is not likely to be one's biological parent: having step-siblings as often

as one has siblings, and having few in either case; spending most of the day, from a very early age until the start of school, in a public day-care institution; having only weak ties to friends and neighbors, maturing extremely quickly . . . .[4]

The Washington Debate

In 1988, pressure again began to build for Congress to revisit the child care issue. A "media blitz" coupled with heavy lobbying from liberal public policy groups led to dozens of bills being introduced in the Congress.

Both Presidential candidates felt compelled to make obligatory visits to child care centers to show their concern about the issue. Curiously, neither candidate took the time to visit a home where a mother was caring for her own children. Such a visit would have sent a powerful message of support for those who have chosen full-time parenting.

By the end of 1988, two clear child care positions had evolved, each representing one of the sides of America's civil war over children. One side favored universal tax credits for all families with children, including stay-at-home mothers. The other side favored government-subsidized child care centers for only those mothers who worked outside the home.

The advocates of Uncle Sam as "national nanny" employed the usual skewed statistics to prove that the great majority of women had already made their choice for child care and that it was up to government to help them. Others actually argued that children were cared for just as well (or even better) by "professionals."

Senator Ted Kennedy, using unsubstantiated numbers, claimed that thousands of women were turning down jobs every day because they couldn't find adequate child care. He chose to ignore dozens of polls and research reports that showed millions of women, particularly in the early years of their children's lives, wanted to be home rather than employed. Unfortunately, these women were driven into the work force against their wishes—often to earn the money needed to pay the increasing tax bill from Uncle Sam.

In 1948, the percentage of income paid in federal taxes by a medium-income family with two children was 2 percent. By 1989 it had risen to 24 percent. Think of it! Millions of mothers have been forced out of the home and away from their children because of the uncontrolled growth of the federal bureaucracy. If Senator Kennedy and his colleagues were so concerned about women, they should have sought ways to lessen this backbreaking tax burden.

The Congress was marching to a different drummer. They first considered an abominable piece of legislation cleverly named Act for Better Child Care (ABC Bill). It was stark in its message about children, values and choices. No church child-care center could receive federal funds unless all sectarian activity ceased in the center. Religious symbols would have to be covered. Lunch-time prayers would be forbidden. The legislation reeked of anti-religious hostility.

If that wasn't outrageous enough, the bill required federal licensing for anyone receiving funds, including grandmothers or relatives, if they were watching the children. And then there was the inevitable kicker: no help was to be provided for the stay-at-home mother. The legislation continued to treat her as a second class citizen.

By the time the legislative process was complete, some of the more onerous provisions had been modified, if for no other reason than the agenda of the cultural elites was too obviously revealed by the bill's provisions. But even after the compromise, the implications for public policy were clear—more discrimination against mothers who cared for their own children, more subsidies for those who selected outside care, more government regulation, more taxation, more efforts to discourage the transmission of religious values, and more discrimination against religious institutions.

In short, more pressure for parents to make choices that Washington bureaucrats and radical feminists preferred. The only kind of child care the bill would subsidize was the variety *least* desired by employed parents: the highly regulated, cookie-cutter standardized, group supervision advocated by the gurus of the child development lobby in university classrooms and Congressional hearing rooms.

At the same time the politicians were pressing for federalized baby-sitting programs, an increasing amount of research was indicating that such care could be very damaging to the children involved.

For example, a study by researchers at the University of Texas at Dallas revealed that children placed in non-maternal care at an early age were less cooperative, less popular, and less confident than their peers. In addition, they had poorer study skills and made lower grades.

Bryna Segal, a developmental psychologist at Stanford University, found that day-care children tended to be more conformist and peer dependent than other children. A study of affluent families in the Chicago area showed that when children less than a year old spent 20 or more hours a week in out-of-home care, they displayed more avoidance of their mothers than those babies cared for by their mothers at home.[5]

Institutional Hazards

The psychological effects of day care are matched by a growing body of evidence indicating significant risk of disease for infants in day care. One recent study by Dr. Ron Haskins and Dr. Jonathan Kotch identified day care attendance as the most significant factor associated with increased incidence of bacterial meningitis. This is not a minor ailment. Ten percent of the children contracting it die, and one-third suffer serious long term physical problems, including blindness and deafness.

Another study corroborated these findings. Infants in day care were over 12 times more likely to become infected with meningitis than home-reared infants. Some studies showed a link between day care and the spread of cytomegalovirus (CMV), the leading cause of congenital infections in newborns, as well as the spread of hepatitis A.

In the case of hepatitis, the research indicates that the incidence of the disease is directly linked to the environment of the child-care center: the younger the children in the center, the more hours each day they are there, and the larger the center, the greater the risk of contagion.[6]

Throughout 1988 and on into 1990, as the child-care debate raged, these studies were seldom if ever mentioned by public policy makers. References to them in the popular media were practically non-existent. TV specials calling for more government support of child-care seldom alluded to the growing body of disturbing evidence on medical implications.

We can't recall one Congressional hearing where the issue was discussed seriously. Even inside the Reagan White House, where a follow-up report on the family was being prepared, there was great reticence to mention the studies. The Bush Administration seems just as hesitant to speak out about this compelling research.

Why? Why were millions of American parents being denied the information they needed to help them make informed choices about the care of their children? Normally, the media would have been crying "censorship." But on the issue of potential damage to children in child-care facilities, there has been a conspiracy of silence.

In one Congressional hearing room, the audience of child-care lobbyists gasped when I suggested that large child-care centers be required to print in their promotional material a notice about the potential health risks to children. Similar warnings are now required on a pack of cigarettes in the name of full disclosure and informed consent. Nevertheless, the Committee ignored my suggestion.

It would be devastating to the feminists and the "national nanny" crowd if there were an informed national debate about the risks of child care. Many American women, already troubled by placing their children in child care, might be tempted to stay at home, particularly in the early years when a child is most vulnerable and parental care most important.

Other parents might look for neighborhood care or supervision by a family member—choices already favored by many parents but frowned upon by the "experts." But little or no debate has taken place on this important issue. Most politicians remain silent, including many who are "pro-family."

Apparently many of them fear that the women whose children are already in child care would be so upset about the information that they would take their anger out against the politician delivering the bad news—instead of against those who originally lured them into the child-care choice in the first place.

Many researchers have been hesitant to do more work in the field. Feminist ire about disturbing studies can be blistering, and researchers brave enough to take on the issue often find themselves under fire on their own university campuses, as well as becoming the targets of public demonstrations. Scholars doing responsible research in these areas also have difficulty publishing their findings in liberal journals.

Public Disinformation

The result of this cowardice and intimidation is that American women have been denied the vital information they need to make the best decisions for their children.

In fact, the feminists and writers who cover popular culture often urge mothers not to worry about the dangers of poor child care. In one popular magazine, the writer quipped, "What if the child-care you find isn't ideal? Well, home life isn't ideal either."[7] This advice must seem particularly flippant for the mother who has experienced the horror of a child molested in a center, or whose children have been exposed to a serious disease.

Efforts to reassure the public about absentee parents have also been evident in the lay press. Notice the blatant disregard of children's welfare in the following editorial by Hyman Rodman:

Forget the Horror Stories about Latchkey Children

We have heard many stories in the media about the terrible things that happen to latchkey children. These reports go beyond the obvious perils of physical harm to the psychological pain suffered by children left alone, such as that of the schoolgirl who cowers in her bedroom closet for two hours until her mother gets home from work. The message that we get is that latchkey children are in grave danger of immediate or long-term harm.

Horror stories about latchkey children make good media copy and sell magazines and books. But horror stories are not scientific evidence. We cannot generalize from anecdotes and incidents. While there have been many studies, dating back to the 1950s on the effect of working mothers on children, we still know very little about the effects of latchkey arrangements on children.

If you have been persuaded by anecdotes that the latchkey arrangement is a serious problem, consider the following: A 10-year-old boy is afraid to return home from school each day, because his mother is at home and she beats him severely. A 9-year-old is so emotionally terrorized by her parents that she hides in her room and avoids them as much as possible. Many children's relationships with their parents are such that they are happiest when they leave for school in the morning and saddest when they return home. Can I now argue that having children go home to waiting parents after school is a terrible arrangement? You would, quite rightly, tell me that such an argument is ridiculous. Yet such generalizations are made about latchkey children, and the media have been swallowing them whole.

Because of the negative connotations that the word *latchkey* has taken on, I prefer to talk about self-care children and self-care arrangements. Clearly the child's age and level of maturity are important considerations in any parent's decision about whether to use the self-care arrangement. The safety of the neighborhood and the availability of nearby help in an emergency are also important considerations. Some parents faced with the cost of child care, or with its limited availability, are turning to self-care as a way out of their dilemma. It serves little purpose to create guilt in these parents by emphasizing the lurking dangers of self-care when we really know so little about the consequences, good or bad.*

This excerpt from a larger editorial takes my breath away. As long as *one* boy or girl is killed or injured in the absence of adult supervision, how can we "forget the horror stories about latchkey children"?

Common sense will tell us that kids can't raise themselves, and that they are extremely vulnerable when left unsupervised. In a day when 20 to 30 percent of all girls and perhaps 10 percent of boys are sexually molested, how can a learned professor tell us to forget the horror stories?

In addition to the potential for exploitation, children are a threat to *themselves and to each other*. Fire, toxic chemicals, falls from trees or windows, dog-bites, and fast moving cars are among the major concerns of parents. How many kids are kidnaped each year? Does Professor Rodman really believe we need to research these dangers in order to validate our concerns about unprotected children?

---

* Hyman Rodman, director of the Family Research Center and the Excellence Foundation Professor in child development and family relations at the University of North Carolina at Greensboro, cited this data in *Family Relations Journal*, January, 1987.

It is this kind of bias from liberal "thinkers" that has characterized the emotional debate about child care and its implications for the next generation. Oh, and by the way, did you notice what Rodman wrote about *parents?* Apparently, they are the greatest threat to children—the only danger we don't need to study.

Now, lest we imply otherwise, we recognize a need for clean, loving, well run child care facilities. Many single mothers, and those at the fringes of poverty, simply must have alternatives for their children while they work outside the home. For those women left with children to raise alone, there is often no other option.

Millions of other women have been told they can—in fact, they must—"have it all" if they are going to be complete modern women. Helen Gurley Brown, editor of *Cosmopolitan* magazine, even wrote a book by that title, *Having It All*. These modern moms are expected to hold down a full-time job, give "quality time" to their children, keep a home, and be as sexy and desirable for their husbands as they were on their wedding day.

Or as Peggy Lee belted out in her classic rendition of "I'm a Woman":

I can rub and scrub till this old house is
shinin' like a dime
Feed the baby, grease the car and powder my
face at the same time
Get all dressed up, go out and swing till four A.M. and then
Lay down at five, jump up at six and start all over again.
Cause I'm a woman.[8]

Some, because of careers, delay childbirth only to find that the biological clock has run out before they have a chance to bring a child into the world. Others have their children but feel compelled to return to work as soon as possible.

In some communities, it has become a status symbol to work as late into the pregnancy as possible and to return to work as soon as possible after birth. Thus, the woman and the child are denied those precious months together when bonding occurs most easily.

In an incredible *Glamour* magazine article—one of the real trendsetters on what modern women are supposed to value and embrace—mothers are warned not to wait too long after the birth of their child to get back to work. Why? Apparently because delay may result in such a bonding (love?) between the new mother and her baby that she will find it too painful to leave. The editors wrote, "Babies are hard to resist once they're at this stage, and mothers can sometimes find it difficult to 'break away' if they delay too long."

In other words, "turn your child over to someone else and get back to the really important things before you get hooked emotionally."

For the hesitant mother, *Glamour* adds this kicker with no evidence to support the assertion: " . . . there's no evidence that exclusive mothering is good for babies."[9]

One renowned researcher, Dr. Burton White, who served as director of the Pre-School Project at Harvard and has devoted a lifetime to studying the early years of a child's life, has made a blunt assessment.

"After more than 30 years of research on how children develop well, I would not think of putting an infant or toddler of my own into any substitute care program on a full time basis, *especially* a center-based *program*."

It is our firm conviction that most mothers don't return to work out of "choice." In many of the nation's larger urban areas, two incomes are needed to access the housing market and pay for the basics.

These two-earner couples face incredible pressures when they start a family. No matter how much we talk about equality, the fact is that mothers and wives bear most of the burden of handling dual responsibilities and most of the guilt falls to them too. Many are torn between the workplace and their natural longings to be with their children.

There is anxiety even in Washington, D.C.—a city that has the highest percentage of mothers working outside the home of any major metropolitan area in America. Yet a *Washington Post* survey showed that 62 percent of those women would be at home with their children *if they could afford it.* A 1986 poll in *Newsweek* confirmed that most mothers working outside of the home would prefer to work fewer hours; and only 13 percent of all working mothers indicated they wanted to work full time.[10]

A recent *USA Today* survey found that 73 percent of all two-parent families would have one parent stay home with children "if money were not an issue." And a recent poll revealed that 84 percent of all employed mothers agree with the statement, "If I could afford it, I would rather be at home with my children."[11]

Whose Little Girl?

My own family has experienced these tensions. Still etched in my memory is a cold, rainy fall day in which my wife Carol and I took our daughter, Elyse, to the house of a wonderful couple who watched our children when we both worked full time.

When Carol returned to the car, tears welled up in her eyes as she told me that Elyse had just greeted the baby-sitter by calling her "mommy." I sat there patiently trying to explain why this episode should not be an occasion for heartbreak. I talked about how the word probably meant nothing more than "female care giver" to our 2 year-old.

I even suggested the episode might reflect how wise we were to have picked a sitter who was showing our child so much love. Carol listened and then demolished all of my rationality with one devastating question. "How would you feel if she called Mike 'Daddy'?" Mike was the sitter's husband and the question drove away any pretense of my objectivity. I looked at Carol and confessed only partly in jest, "It would kill me."

We drove to our jobs in Washington that morning mostly in silence. Whether we realized it or not, that day we began a process that would end with Carol rejecting a career for now and fully embracing motherhood. We have been able to live on my income, but millions of other families need the woman's salary. Still other mothers working outside the home can't bring themselves to buck the popular culture that tells them in a million ways that a career is more important than raising a child.

Many women must deal with frustration in the workplace as well as the problems of having too little time left for real nurturing. For millions of American women, life has become a never-ending treadmill.

For those women who do choose to stay home for a few years (or possibly longer) after the baby comes, they often experience isolation and a vague sense of cultural censure. They can't help wondering if they are missing something in the fast-paced, exciting business world. They wonder whether their education isn't being wasted because they are merely raising children.

These women see their neighbors with two incomes enjoying a higher standard of living, a newer car in their driveway, more frequent vacations, and they begin to wonder if they're not "suckers" hanging on to an out-dated lifestyle that the media denigrates and most politicians give only the slightest lip service.

While they perform the most important job in any culture—the care and nurturing of the next generation of citizens—they somehow are made to feel wasted and useless. And then, as the ultimate insult, government enters the picture and says such families will be taxed in order to help pay the child-care expenses of two-income families.

It is not surprising that many women are growing tired of being expected to do the impossible. For those who want to work outside the home, an increasing number are working part-time to free up more hours with their children.

According to the Bureau of Labor Statistics, the number of women working part-time increased 31 percent between 1976 and 1986. Many women are coming to the same conclusion as one new mother looking for child-care. She spent hours crafting the descriptions of the person she wanted to care for her child when suddenly she had a startling insight.

> My carefully worded advertisements for child care literally came back to haunt me . . . I wanted someone who would encourage my children's creativity, take them on interesting outings, answer all their little questions, and rock them to sleep. I wanted someone who would be a "part of the family."
>
> Slowly, painfully, after really thinking about what I wanted for my children and rewriting advertisement after advertisement, I came to the stunning realization that the person I was looking for was right under my nose. I had been desperately trying to hire me.[12]

Government policy ought not to tilt the playing field against the natural desire of such mothers to spend more time with their children. And government bureaucrats should be given a clear message to keep their noses out of the nursery.

No Substitute for Mother's Love

No governmental bureaucracy, no matter how decent, no matter how caring, no matter how democratic, and no matter how well funded, can supply the attention and love that children need and that only parents can provide. If social and economic trends deprive children of their parents, government and all other institutions would be overwhelmed with the impossible job of civilizing the next generation.

Any involvement by Washington in child care should follow some clear principles. First it must not be discriminatory. American families are laboring under an incredible tax burden. To ease that burden, higher tax credits for each child ought to be implemented immediately. Each family can then make their own decisions about whether to use the credit for outside child care or to help pay their other bills so that the mother who wants to stay home can do so.

In the Tax Reform Act of 1986, the dependents' deduction was raised from $1,000 to nearly $2,000 for each child. It ought to be increased again to $7,000 in order to lessen the economic pressure on families with children. This is not a radical proposal. It would merely return the average family to the level of taxes that families enjoyed at the end of World War II, when corrected for inflation.

Second, parents who choose church-based child care, or parents who prefer to have an extended family member or small home-based center care for their children, should receive the same benefits as those selecting large, secular, for-profit child care centers. Parents shouldn't be discouraged from looking for care that most resembles the supervision the child would receive in his own home.

Other things can be done. While some deregulation has taken place, more is needed to enable those who want to, to work from their homes. The fast growth of the computer revolution will increase the opportunity for this "home-work" option in the future, allowing more parents to be at home with their children.

These changes in government regulations, tax laws, and child-care policies are important. But nothing is as significant as rediscovering as a nation the importance of mothers and providing them with the emotional support they need to raise children effectively.

Author Brenda Hunter, writing about the "power of mother love," referred to John Merrick, the hideously deformed man afflicted with elephantiasis. Anthropologist Ashly Montagu, in a book entitled *The Elephant Man*, described Merrick's life in a carnival side show where people paid to view his monstrous head. Merrick was not retarded, but he was aware of his grotesque appearance and fully understood the horror people felt when they saw him. The mental pain he suffered must have been incredible.

If anyone had a right to be filled with hate, hostility and anti-social sentiment, it would have been Merrick. Yet Sir Frederick Treves who befriended him found that Merrick "had passed through the fire and come out unscathed. His troubles had enabled him. He showed himself to be a gentle, affectionate and lovable creature . . . free from any trace of cynicism or resentment."

How could this be? Montagu believed it was because Merrick received from his mother the love and warmth that protected him from developing the deformed personality to match his deformed body.[13]

A mother's love is the common currency that not only enables individuals to resist a slide into madness and anti-social behavior but also permits civilization to prevail from one generation to the next. Without it we are doomed as a people and a nation.

If we believe that to be true, our public policy should reflect our commitment to motherhood.

Gary L. Bauer

8

BEHOLD, I SET
BEFORE YOU LIFE
...AND DEATH

Out of That Darkness . . . Toward That Light

One of the most fascinating books I have ever read is *Witness*, the memoirs of Whittaker Chambers, a communist agent who eventually rejected Marxism and opted for liberty. One of the turning points in his life that led to his rejection of communism took place in October of 1933 when Chambers discovered his wife was pregnant.

Many of his fellow communists believed that it was morally wrong for a professional revolutionary to have children at all. Chambers assumed that his wife would abort the baby. But in a chapter only six pages long, simply titled *The Child*, Chambers writes that his baby was saved. He says,

> My wife came over to me, took my hands and burst into tears. "Dear heart," she said in a pleading voice, "we couldn't do that awful thing to a little baby, not to a little

baby, dear heart." A wild joy swept me. Reason, the agony of my family, the Communist Party and its theories, the wars and revolutions of the 20th century, crumbled at the touch of the child.

Later after the baby was born Chambers wrote:

I went back to my wife who was no longer only my wife but the mother of our child—the child we all yearn for, who, even before her birth, had begun, invisibly, to lead us out of that darkness, which we could not even realize, toward that light, which we could not even see.[1]

One of the hottest battlegrounds in America's current civil war focuses on the worth and value of human life. The conflict extends from one end of human existence to the other. Both pre-born children and aging invalids are at risk. This is not merely a debate over words. The casualties in this battle are real and immediate. On one side are those who believe in the universal sanctity of human life. Arrayed against them are those who argue for a "quality of life" ethic.

Not coincidentally, the issue of abortion most resembles the other issue that led our forefathers to literally take up arms against each other—the question of slavery. In many crucial ways, abortion and slavery are not merely similar issues—they are the same issue.

Abortion and Slavery

The original contract of our nation's founding—the core document that defines who we are—is the Declaration of Independence. It is in the words of the Declaration that our founding fathers proclaimed the self-evident truths that led us to take up arms and break away to form a separate independent nation.

Of these truths, the most central is embodied in this simple but powerful sentence: "all men are created equal," that they are endowed by their Creator with "certain unalienable Rights," and that among these rights are "life, liberty and the pursuit of happiness." This is the American creed—a basic truth that is the foundation of our liberty.

But every school child knows that from the very birth of our nation, the Constitution permitted a contradiction to these clear words. Faced with the need to build a nation composed of states with different economic and social needs, the founders permitted slavery to continue so that the slave states could be brought into the Union. We can debate their pragmatism, but one thing was clear to many of the founders, and it became painfully more obvious with each passing year: this contradiction between the principles of the Declaration and the fact of sanctioned slavery could not exist forever. "A house divided cannot stand."

The history books reflecting on that era tell a story of a country trying to hide from that basic truth. Either the nation would be all slave, and the spirit of our Declaration turned into mere words, or it would be all free whatever price had to be paid.

In 1857, the United States Supreme Court in one of its most shameful moments decided in the Dred Scott case that slavery was permissible. That decision declared that a Black slave was not a person under the Constitution but mere property whose future depended on the whims of its owner. "A Black man has no right which the white man is bound to respect," said Chief Justice Roger B. Taney.

As in many other times of crisis, America was blessed in that day by the life of a great man willing to speak the truth about the horror of slavery and of the Supreme Court decision that ratified it. Abraham Lincoln, the Great Emancipator, spoke plainly: "If slavery is not wrong, then nothing is wrong." Even though the implications for his own political future were unclear, Lincoln used moral persuasion to convince his fellow Americans that the nation was abandoning its commitment to the equality and worth of all human life.

In one of his famous debates with Senator Stephen Douglas, Lincoln said ". . . eighty years ago we began by declaring all men equal, but now (as steadily as a man's march to the grave) we have run down to that other declaration, that for some men to enslave others is a sacred right of government. These principles cannot stand together. They are as opposite as God and Mammon, and whoever holds to the one must despise the other." Ultimately, it took Lincoln's inspired words plus the lives of 600,000 of our forefathers to help the nation to reaffirm that *all* men are created equal.

Roe v. Wade

Once again, a Supreme Court of the United States was called upon in 1973 to defend an unprotected minority that was being deprived of life itself. And in the tradition of the Dred Scott case, it failed the test.

The Supreme Court, in the *Roe v. Wade* decision, struck down in one stroke every state law restricting abortion. Some of our conservative friends were outraged then and remain agitated today that the Court in its decision violated the rules of federalism—the idea that each state must be able to make its own laws, consistent with the Constitution. But they miss the larger point.

The Dred Scott case excluded Blacks from the protections granted by the Declaration. The *Roe v. Wade* case did the same for our unborn children. Justice Harry Blackmun wrote in his opinion, "We need not decide the difficult question of when human life begins." But, of course, that is exactly what the court had to decide. If the child in his mother's womb is human, and surely he can be nothing else, then the rights affirmed by the Declaration and given by God must not be taken away.

For nearly two decades, the most defenseless among us have had rights only if they were "wanted" by the mother who carried them. Otherwise they are mere property to be disposed of for whatever reason, or for no reason. And in those intervening years, nearly 25 million unborn babies have been disposed of—victims of our society's worship of choice and rampant individualism. Under *Roe,* an unborn child has no rights anyone is bound to respect.

Again over 100 years ago, Lincoln saw the danger of this selective granting of rights. He asked:

> I should like to know if taking this old Declaration of Independence, which declares that all men are equal upon principle and making exceptions to it where will it stop. If one man says it does not mean a negro, why not another say it does not mean some other man?

Today Lincoln might have asked, if the Declaration does not apply to the unborn child, then why can't another man say it doesn't cover a handicapped newborn child or the terminally ill or the handicapped? But that is exactly what has happened.

With each passing day, the process of taking the right to life from one individual or another because someone declares them unwanted or a burden or not possessing a sufficient quality of life has broadened and accelerated. In 1983 the state courts of Indiana allowed the starvation death of "Baby Doe" in Bloomington because the child had Down's Syndrome.

No one argued about whether Baby Doe was a human being. Unlike the invisible baby in the womb, this infant was born and there for all of us, including wise judges, to see. The issue at stake was whether this handicapped baby had a right to medical treatment to preserve his life.

The decision of the judges was a triumph for the quality of life over the sanctity of life. Baby Doe committed no transgression. His only mistake was to have the misfortune of being born in a society with not enough love to go around. Today we believe he sits on the right hand of the One who said, "I was hungry and you gave me food, I was thirsty and you gave me drink, I was a stranger and you welcomed me."

Who Lives? Who Dies?

In Oklahoma, a team of physicians conducted a grotesque experiment on newborn handicapped children, representing the triumph of the quality of life ethic. Over a five year period, the physicians decided which infants suffering from spina bifida—an imperfect closure of part of the spinal column—would live and which would die.

The criteria used by the medical team to decide who would survive included a formula whose purpose was intended to predict the quality of life of the child if it were allowed to grow up. Items in the formula included the child's intellectual and physical endowments, how much society would likely have to contribute to raising the child, and the economic status of the family. In other words, babies from poor families were denied medical treatment.

Of the 69 babies in the "study," 24 received the minimal treatment and all of them died. The remaining children received full treatment and all of them lived. In other words, a team of doctors took upon themselves the right to play God.

There have been other dramatic examples of the cheapening of life in Western Society. Evidence grows that some women have obtained (and continue to obtain) abortions because they were unhappy with the sex of their unborn child. By an overwhelming margin, the defenseless babies being aborted in these cases were female! What a twist of a "woman's right."

The Family Research Council has urged the Justice Department to investigate whether civil rights laws are being violated by such abortions. We asked Molly Yard and the National Organization of Women to join us in the complaint. They never responded. Apparently, abortion is satisfactory to some feminists if it is intended to eliminate baby girls!

It is difficult to imagine a more evil development in our society. We only have to look at the outcome of a similar philosophy that took root in Germany and ended with the horror of the "final solution to the Jewish problem." This downward slide was explained dramatically by Dr. Leo Alexander in an article in the *New England Journal of Medicine*, written in 1949.

Dr. Alexander was a consultant to the Secretary of War in the Nuremberg Trials. He had extraordinary access to accused Nazi war criminals in the medical community. Writing from that unique perspective, Dr. Alexander argued that so-called "compassionate killing" of the terminally ill inevitably set the stage for the Holocaust. He wrote:

> Whatever proportions these crimes finally assumed, it became evident to all who investigated them that they had started from small beginnings. The beginnings at first were merely a subtle shift in emphasis in the basic attitude of the physicians. It started with the acceptance of the attitude . . . that there is such a thing as life not worthy to be lived. This attitude in its early stages concerned itself merely with the severely and chronically sick. Gradually the sphere of those to be included in this category was enlarged to encompass the socially unproductive, the ideologically unwanted, the racially unwanted and finally all non-Germans.[2]

Before his death, Dr. Alexander told a friend that trends in our country were "much like Germany in the '20s and '30s. The barriers against killing are coming down."[3]

The same *New England Journal of Medicine* in which 50 years ago Dr. Alexander wrote his original warning presents evidence of the cheapening of human life. On April 12, 1984, Dr. Sidney Wanzer, a board member of the Society for the Right to Die, joined by nine prominent colleagues, wrote a commentary entitled, "The Physician's Responsibility Toward Hopelessly Ill Patients."

In it, the doctors from leading institutions such as Harvard and Johns Hopkins called for the cessation of "artificially administered nutritional support, including fluids, from various kinds of patients, such as those seriously and irreversibly demented."

On January 8, 1988, the *Journal of the American Medical Association* published an anonymous article entitled "It's Over Debbie." In this piece, a physician gives his account of the lethal injection he administered at the request of a young woman terminally ill with cancer. In March of 1989, 10 influential physicians on a panel chaired by Daniel Federman of Harvard Law School, called for "wide and open discussion" of "assisted suicide," and while admitting the subject was "complex," assured readers that all but two of the doctors believe "it is not immoral."

More recently, Marcia Angell, the Executive Editor of the *New England Journal of Medicine,* was quoted as saying, "I think perhaps we're ready to consider euthanasia that is very, very strictly controlled."

Polling data indicates these attitudes are not limited to a fringe of the medical community. Seventy percent of physicians polled in San Francisco said they thought incurable patients should be able to request euthanasia and 45 percent said they would be willing to carry it out.

A Colorado survey showed 59 percent of doctors in that state would be willing to give patients a lethal drug if it were legal. Efforts are underway in several states to legalize euthanasia by putting initiatives on the state ballot. A failed effort to do this in California collected over 130,000 signatures in favor of the initiative. Its proponents reportedly plan another attempt soon. This time they will *start* with 130,000 computerized names and addresses.[4]

In a recent book entitled *Setting Limits,* Dr. Daniel Callahan, one of America's leading bioethicists, has actually suggested that upon reaching a certain age, the elderly "have no right to burden the public purse." The doctor has suggested the ideal age would be between 80–85.[5] But someone else may believe the age should be 75 or 70. And if 70, why not 69, or 50, or 40 or . . . 18?

Once the door marked "death" is open, it does not close easily. Joseph Fletcher, a theologian, has suggested that infants may be killed if they don't measure up to fifteen "indicators of personhood."[6] The sanctity of life ethic protects us all; the quality of life ethic will ultimately protect none of us.

The law has already been changed in the Netherlands. Doctors now actually make house calls to assist patients in dying at their own hands. Some estimate that as many as 5,000 Dutch citizens die this way each year—always at their own request and "choice," of course. But the line between choice and compulsion is thin.

One critic of the Dutch program says that "Dutch society has so emphasized the duty of the hopelessly ill to forego treatment" that they feel compelled to ask to be killed. "Elderly people begin to consider themselves a burden to society . . . under an obligation to start conversations on euthanasia, or even to request it."[7] Down the slippery slope they went.

Both the abortion issue and the related question of euthanasia are the subjects of legal maneuvering and court battles. Millions of Americans celebrated when the Supreme Court, in July, 1989, for the first time since 1973, began to undermine the unrestricted right to abortion. But the celebration should be muted, for in this narrow victory there was no language that went to the heart of the issue— the Constitutional protection of life.

Even on the current "conservative" court, there may only be two or three justices at most who are willing to extend the protections of the Declaration of Independence and the Constitution to all Americans, including the unborn.

But whatever the courts do, they are only part of the civil war raging over the issue of life and death. What is loose in our society is a philosophy promoted by the cultural elites that goes to the very heart of the nature of our nation and even of Western civilization.

Either as a society we will believe and teach our children that life is always sacred, or we will believe and teach that it has no intrinsic value aside from what we assign to it. Like the other issues at stake in the conflict, the answer cannot embrace both philosophies. Either one will prevail or the other.

The wording of our Declaration of Independence leaves no doubt that life is always sacred, but in the name of progress or science, we have retreated far from that clear understanding today. Regardless of the outcome of pending court cases, this battle will be won by the side that is able to win the hearts and minds of their fellow citizens.

Malcolm Muggeridge, who has received world fame as a lecturer and broadcaster, described the choice this way:

> Which vision are we for? On the one hand, as the pattern of our collective existence, the broiler house or factory farm, in which the concern is solely for the physical well-being of the livestock and the financial well-being of the enterprise; on the other, mankind as a family, all of whose members, whatever physical or mental qualities or deficiencies they may have, are equally deserving of consideration in the eyes of their creator, and whose existence has validity, not just in itself, nor just in relation to history, but in relation to

a destiny reaching beyond time and into eternity. Or in simple terms, on the one hand the quality of life; on the other, the sanctity of life.[8]

A Personal Note

A woman I never met has had a tremendous impact on me. In fact, I would not be alive today if it weren't for her courage. Whether she was a scared teenager, rich or poor, will be forever hidden from me. All I know is that she decided to give birth to my father in 1914 and place him in an orphanage.

My father had a hard life during those early years. He was in and out of foster care but finally was adopted, unfortunately, into a family which abused him. He fell into the grip of alcoholism as a young man and wrestled with it on and off the rest of his days.

He was never quite able to understand why he had been abandoned by his birth parents. Some of the most painful moments I have experienced were those times as a young boy when I watched my father weep for the parents that he never knew.

In the depths of the Great Depression, Dad dropped out of school to find work to help his family. As a result, he enjoyed none of the financial success our society emphasizes these days. His lack of education and a persistent battle with alcoholism limited his working years to a series of low-paying blue-collar jobs. But he always worked no matter how menial the task and, out of pride, never considered taking any government handout, although our family would certainly have qualified. What little we did have was always shared—with the church and with those in our own neighborhood who had even less.

Many today would argue that Stanley "Spike" Bauer would have been better off to have never been born at all. No doubt there were times when he would have agreed. But with all the odds against him, he did manage to accomplish a lot in his life. He met a sweet 17-year-old girl who would become my mother. He married her and they were husband and wife until he passed away 49 years later.

My father understood honor and duty. He volunteered for the Marines in World War II, served in the South Pacific, was wounded in action and saved the lives of two buddies in the heat of battle. He received two purple hearts and a bronze star for bravery under fire. Returning home traumatized by the horror of war, he remained haunted by dark dreams of death and destruction.

My mother tolerated much and no doubt saved my father from a life in the gutter. Together they bought a home, paid their taxes, had a son, introduced me to the saving power of faith and taught me that if I worked hard enough, anything was possible. When I was 13 years old and I accepted the forgiveness of Christ, the footsteps I heard behind me as I walked to the front of the church were those of my Dad. We were baptized together, a memory I will keep with me always.

I left home to go to Washington, D.C. in 1969 to attend law school. By 1987 my father's son had become the Senior Domestic Policy Advisor to the President of the United States.

Now the cycle continues. God has given my wife and me three children who are filled with dreams and potential. I cannot know what happiness or suffering lies ahead for them or for myself. None of us can see the future. But I do know that life is a precious gift from God—that life is better than the culture of death which has taken so many unborn children from us.

Would some of the babies aborted since 1973 have been "crack" babies? Would some have been poor? Would some have been burdens on society? The answer is yes to all three questions. Does that mean they do not have a right to life? The answer is no.

Some of these children, perhaps many, would have overcome these obstacles and given us gifts we can only vaguely imagine. If that young girl many years ago had chosen death, my father would have never been born. And without his life and my mother's, mine would have been impossible. And without Carol and me, Elyse, Sarah, and Zachary would never have come into the world.

Along with millions of other Americans, my family's favorite movie is the Frank Capra classic, *It's a Wonderful Life,* starring Jimmy Stewart as George Baily—a big-hearted, "aw shucks" kind of guy who was always sacrificing for others.

As anyone who has seen the movie knows, George falls on hard times and is tempted to take his own life. Standing on a snowswept bridge he wishes he had never been born. A bumbling guardian angel trying to earn his wings is sent by God to try to show George just why his life had been important.

This angel, named Clarence, first shows George what the world would have been like without him. Then Clarence summarizes the moral of the movie: "Strange, isn't it? Every man's life touches so many other lives, and when he isn't around he leaves an awful hole to fill, doesn't he? . . . You see what a mistake it would be to throw it away?"

"An awful hole to fill . . ." What kind of hole have we created by aborting 25 million babies? What promises are unfulfilled in those tiny innocent lives we've snuffed out? Have we killed the child who would someday find a cure for cancer or AIDS? How many composers, writers, statesmen will never have a chance to live their lives? But just as important, how many common men and women have been eliminated who may have done nothing more than overcome the odds and escape poverty, or a handicap, or disease, to have their own family and bring other children into the world? Only God knows.

A President's Tears

The Cabinet Room at the White House is impressive. Outside the windows on one side of the room are the carefully manicured White House gardens. In the room itself, large portraits of former Presidents bedeck the walls. In the winter, the White House staff used to build a crackling fire in the large fireplace at one end of the room. At the other end, another door opens to the short passageway to the Oval Office. The momentous decisions and discussions that have taken place in the Cabinet room fill volumes of history books.

I remember one event that I don't believe has been recorded anywhere else—and yet it symbolizes the great challenge facing our nation.

On Mondays, when the President's schedule allowed, the senior members of the White House staff would have lunch with Mr. Reagan in the Cabinet room. It was usually a relaxed time. The President would let his hair down and his Irish humor would begin to go into high gear. No press was permitted at these sessions. It was a special time and an important moment away from the glare of the usually present cameras.

Normally our talk was about grand legislative and strategy issues. But I always found the President was more comfortable talking about real live people than arcane Washington maneuverings. One day as we went around the table to take turns raising issues with the President, I chose to read to him a few paragraphs from a *Newsday* story about a little four-year-old girl.

The story was titled, "Baby Doe's Success: Progress defying prognosis." I read the President the opening paragraphs which said in part,

> Keri-Lynn talks and laughs; she smiles and hugs and screams and plants kisses firmly on a stranger's cheek.

She has recently begun to demand more than her share and often resorts to throwing toys or M&Ms when the focus shifts away from her. Then she whispers, "I'm bad," aware that her mother is displeased with her behavior.

"Sit down," Keri-Lynn ordered a visitor last Wednesday night, while demanding that her mother, Linda, bring her a pack of crayons. Later, she whispered, "Dance, Daddy, dance," as her father swept her into his arms to sway to the music of Stevie Wonder.

For most 4-year-olds, those would not be unusual feats. But for Keri-Lynn, daughter of Dan and Linda A., those are actions doctors thought she would never be able to perform.

Just after she was born, doctors said that Keri-Lynn— better known as Long Island's Baby Jane Doe—would never know happiness and would experience only pain. They said she would be bedridden for life, probably unaware of who her parents were. And she was not expected to talk or walk.

But now Keri-Lynn, age 4, wears a white nightgown trimmed in pink and green with a cap of dark brown curls framing her slate-blue eyes. And she demands, in a hushed but firm tone, "Hug me."[9]

I waited a moment watching the President closely and then I told him the good news. "Mr. President, I thought you would want to know about Keri-Lynn. Four years ago when she was born with multiple birth defects, your Administration went to court to obtain her medical records because of reports she was not receiving equal medical treatment with 'normal' children.

"In short, some thought she should be allowed to die. As you will recall, Mr. President, we lost the case; but even though we didn't even know the child's name or her parents, they decided to ignore the medical advice and do everything they could to save her. Mr. President, I believe this child is alive today because of the courage of her parents and your courage in taking on the medical establishment."

I paused and waited for the President's reaction. I knew he would be happy, but an extraordinary thing happened at that moment. The President wept. All of us with various degrees of embarrassment watched tears well-up in his eyes. He quickly wiped them away and expressed his gratitude to me for sharing the story.

We went on to other issues that day as we always did. But for a brief moment one of the most powerful men in the world had cried over one little four-year-old who was born on October 11, 1983. A four-year-old born with spina bifida (an open spine), an abnormally small head, excess fluid on the brain, and a damaged kidney. No cameras recorded the moment when the President shed those tears, but it will always remain with me as one of the most vivid memories I have of Ronald Wilson Reagan and the kind of man he is.

But it also left me with a lasting impression. If he could be so moved by the story of this struggling little four-year-old who was defying the odds, couldn't we as a nation find enough love to go around for all of America's abandoned children—the crack babies, the fatherless kids wandering our city streets, the unborn children who will be torn to pieces, the teenagers sucked into the drug culture or enticed into sex without love or marriage or commitment?

We adults have come up with a thousand ways in the last 20 years to "fulfill" ourselves, to reach our potential, and to "grow" but we are losing our children in the process. Unless we can rediscover the passion behind that President's tears and turn it into a national commitment to save the young from the forces loose in our secular age, this special experiment in liberty under God is destined to fail. And we will not only suffer the verdict of history, but we must also answer to that just and loving God from whom each of these children came as His precious gifts of life.

9

MOTHERS AND FATHERS

There are exceptional women, there are exceptional men, who have other tasks to perform in addition to the task of motherhood and fatherhood, the task of providing for the home and of keeping it. But it is the tasks connected with the home that are the fundamental tasks of humanity. . . . if the mother does not do her duty, there will either be no next generation, or a next generation that is worse than none at all. . . .

Theodore Roosevelt

It is hard to imagine an American political leader today articulating as clear a defense of the "profession" of parenting as Teddy Roosevelt did earlier in this century. In recent years our culture has sent hostile signals about the job of parenting even though few men and women will ever do anything more important than nurturing and raising the next generation of children.

With mothering and fathering under such fierce attack, it should not be surprising that millions of Americans have brought children into the world and then retreated from parenting. The consequences for many of our sons and daughters is devastating. In the final analysis, I fear that America's "parent deficit" will soon dwarf its "trade deficit" in significance.

Motherhood Under Siege

The vanguard of the attack against mothers was led by the troops of the feminist movement in the '60s and '70s. Militant feminists argued that the job of caring for children was a form of oppression, slavery, or imprisonment. Some feminists compared the mental state of homemakers to soldiers in World War II who had suffered severe emotional damage in combat.

In 1970, Germaine Greer wrote *The Female Eunuch* which condemned motherhood as a handicap and pregnancy as an illness. Greer urged women to be "deliberately promiscuous" and to be certain not to conceive children. Broadening her attack against the whole institution of marriage, she concluded, "If women are to effect a significant amelioration in their condition, it seems obvious that they must refuse to marry."[1]

The classic critique on motherhood and family was Betty Friedan's, *The Feminine Mystique*. Friedan described the family as an oppressive institution. She compared homemakers to "parasites" and said that sexist ideas were "burying millions of American women alive."[2]

Not surprisingly, this anti-mother/anti-family rhetoric disgusted millions of American women, including many who were sympathetic to some feminist goals. The rejection of motherhood helped to derail the movement as a political force in the '80s. But today, the hostility to motherhood is no longer limited to the feminist fringe. Like so many other attacks on traditional institutions, this one has been embraced by the cultural elites and has become their established worldview.

The message that is being sent from the media, government, judges, Madison Avenue, and Hollywood is that parenting is a second-class occupation, best left to those who really can't do anything else.

On our most hallowed university campuses, young women are being taught that "real women" aren't just mothers and homemakers any more. When First Lady Barbara Bush was invited, in 1990, to give the commencement address at Wellesley College, hundreds of angry coeds protested. They argued that Mrs. Bush wasn't a suitable role model for young women because she had spent her life raising children rather than pursuing a career for herself. These students are supposed to be America's "best and brightest" women. What does their protest say about the value they place on caring for children or on children themselves?

Hopefully, they listened carefully to the First Lady's words. She courageously spoke up for family and parenting. She told them,

> The . . . choice that must not be missed is to cherish your human connections: your relationships with friends and family. For several years, you've had impressed upon you the importance to your career of dedication and hard work. This is true, but as important as your obligations as a doctor, lawyer, or business leader will be, you are a human being first and those human connections—with spouses, with children, with friends—are the most important investments you will ever make.
>
> At the end of your life, you will never regret not having passed one more test, not winning one more verdict or not closing one more deal. You will regret time not spent with a husband, a friend, a child or a parent.

This is common sense advice, but it contradicts the anti-mothering bias that exists in our culture. Unbelievably, some so-called "experts" on the family are now arguing that the maternal instinct does not even exist.

A few days after the *New York Times* ran an article about how "drugs" killed the maternal instinct and led to child abuse, they received a lengthy letter from an assistant professor of anthropology at Colorado College. The learned Professor wrote:

> To my knowledge there is no objective substantiation of a maternal instinct in female human beings. The reasoning not only generates a mechanical fix-it mentality but also implies something specifically vulnerable and dangerous about women in this society.[3]

Can you imagine what our sons and daughters are learning in that professor's classroom? The maternal instinct does not make women "vulnerable" nor is it "dangerous." What is dangerous is the constant devaluing of the job of caring for and nurturing children.

Politicians and government bureaucrats often have their own warped ideas about mothering. During the 1988 campaign, Democratic Presidential nominee Mike Dukakis participated in a "round table" discussion on health insurance at a Houston hospital. He turned to a woman there with her husband and three children aged 10, 7 and 4. "Do you work?" Dukakis asked the mother. With some emotion the woman replied, "I take care of my children. I work very hard." A chastened Dukakis sheepishly said, "That was a dumb question."[4]

Yes it was—but it reflected the tenor of the times.

Who Deserves a Break?

The Reagan Administration also revealed at times these subtle prejudices against at-home mothers. In early 1988, the Administration attempted to develop a child care policy to counter legislation in Congress that would turn Uncle Sam into the national nanny. There was a bruising fight within the White House itself on what our approach should be. I argued for basic fairness—give every family with children under a certain age a tax credit—including stay-at-home mothers. Let them spend the money the way they see fit.

The fight came to a head at a meeting of White House staff and sub-Cabinet officials in the Roosevelt Room. Not surprisingly, many of the participants were women. Unfortunately, most of them favored child care grants but only for families whose children were being cared for outside the home.

I patiently argued the case for fairness to at-home mothers, but my patience evaporated when a government bureaucrat said, "Why should some woman *who is not doing anything* be given a grant or tax break?"

Not doing anything? My wife was at home with our children. I saw the exhaustion in her face when I would come home for dinner. Anyone who has raised a child knows it is a tough, challenging, and often frustrating job, interrupted by moments of unsurpassed joy. Our country will rise or fall depending on whether or not the next generation will be raised with the love and attention they need. "Not doing anything?" I was incensed by the speaker's ignorance: these women are doing the most important job in the world!

As I glanced around the table I suddenly realized an extraordinary fact. Of the eight women in the room—none of them had children! Only a few were married. Yet here they were making child-care policy for the American family and expounding on motherhood.

The bias against stay-at-home moms even makes it to the comic pages. I recall one episode in the "Marvin" comic, which runs in many major papers including the *Washington*

Post. This day, Marvin was shown asking another baby, "Molly, do you have a working mother . . . or a full-time lackey?"

The subtle messages received from the culture, particularly by our children, send a clear message about marriage and parenting. A Saturday morning TV commercial promoting a fast food restaurant shows a group of children sharing hamburgers and french fries while they discuss what they are going to do when they become adults. One child after another, boy and girl, mentions exciting occupations. The only negative reaction is reserved for the boy who says he wants to get married!

Shopping recently at a local "super mall," I saw one of those incidents that seemed to symbolize the clashing values in our culture. A child in the crowded store I was in had inadvertently stepped on the foot of a young woman shopper. The incident quickly escalated into some heated words between the young woman and the child's parents, who had three other children all appearing to be under the age of eight or so.

The yuppie shopper ended the exchange with an extraordinary verbal attack. "Why don't you two practice some birth control?" she screamed. Several other shoppers snickered at this remark and the couple with their four children in tow scurried away. The mother, in particular, looked as though a dagger had just been plunged into her heart.

What an extraordinary incident to witness. Yet it is not really that unusual except for its bluntness. Several acquaintances of ours with more than the national average of 2.3 children have shared incidents of similar hostility. Four children seems to be the anger point. Not many years ago a couple deciding by choice to have no children or only one child was vaguely perceived as being a little unusual. Today, even though the American birthrate is below replacement level, there is still an aversion to large families in some circles.

A recent Focus on the Family radio broadcast featured Randy and Marcia Hekman, who are parents of ten delightful children. The program focused on the joys and stresses of raising a large family. The vast majority of radio listeners that day loved the discussion, based on the mail response.

Dr. Dobson was surprised, however, to receive at least 20 letters from people who resented the Hekmans and their large family. "No one should have the right to have that many children," they chided. Randy and Marcia said they run into similar attitudes quite frequently. Apparently some of the critics would favor a law prohibiting large families in the future. The Hekmans sometimes cry when they remember that they almost decided not to have the fifth and subsequent children.

He Says Children Are the Problem

This hostility to children in society was obvious in another meeting I had at the White House with a prominent California politician. This man was known for his intellect and was considered to be a good bet for higher office down the road. After a half hour or so of talking about a variety of urban problems, he suddenly lowered his voice and said he had been playing around with a new idea for some time. He realized it would be controversial, but he wanted to run it past me confidentially. I agreed to listen with an open mind.

My visitor then suggested that major U.S. pharmaceutical companies be approached and asked to develop a contraceptive chemical that could be put in the water supply of our major cities! I was stunned. "But what about couples who want to have a child?" I inquired. "Oh that's simple," he replied. "They would go to the government and if we felt they were suitable parents we would give them the antidote that would permit them to conceive. Children are the problem," he said. "There are just too darn many children."

I assume he meant too many children born out of wedlock, too many children born to drug addicted parents, too many children born with the AIDS virus. That these are tragedies and burdens to society cannot be doubted. But, a return to moral common sense, a return to self-restraint and responsibility, and a rebirth of compassion, together could do much about overcoming our problems.

Apparently that idea was too radical for my guest. Faced with problems caused at least in part by government bungling and cultural drift, combined with progressive moral decay, this politician's answer was a government solution that would strike an unbelievably stupid blow at the family.

Anti-family bias even finds its way into our schools. One researcher examined ten sets of textbooks used in elementary schools throughout the country. He found there was hardly a story that celebrated motherhood or marriage as a positive goal or as a rich and meaningful way of living. Motherhood was portrayed in two or three stories positively, but these were set in the past or involved an ethnic emphasis that distanced the mother from contemporary American life. No story showed any woman or girl with a positive relationship to a baby or a young child.[5]

Textbook publishers understand what they must do to prevent becoming a target of protests by radical feminists. The guidelines of one major textbook publisher warn authors and illustrators to avoid material that "reinforces any sense that girls and boys may have of being categorized as a sex group." In fact,

> . . . riffling through the pages of your daughter's school books what you won't see (or your daughters either) is a single image celebrating the work women do as wives and mothers. That information, a whole area of sexual life is carefully and systematically expunged from the official cultural record.[6]

Censorship is apparently okay just so long as the right censors are in control!

Even our federal courts have sent a clearly negative message about parenting. Supreme Court Justice Harry Blackmun has written that the Court is interested in questions of marriage, family, and childhood only to the extent that they bear upon the freedom of the individual. The Justice ignores any concept of the public good or the contribution to society that individuals make through the nurture and training of the next generation, or through maintaining the institution of marriage and commitment to one's spouse. Alas, Blackmun's reasoning should not be surprising when one remembers that he is the principal author of the *Roe v. Wade* decision that legalized abortion on demand.

A recent Gallup poll found that only one third of parents nationwide felt that society puts a great deal of value on children while fully 20 percent felt that our culture puts *little value* on children. Is it any wonder that so many women delay having children, or that those who do tend to feel isolated and alone, particularly when they give up a career in order to care for their children? Our culture has made these young mothers victims of a pre-programmed guilt trip.

Some of the anti-utopian science fiction of the last several decades deals with an imaginary dark world in the future where motherhood has been abandoned to technology and the state. In the novel *We,* published in 1924, a world is portrayed in which the very word "family" has come to be regarded as "the language of our ancestors." But the main character of this work instinctively misses the bond of his mother, not really understanding what he is missing.[7]

A World Without Mothers

A world without mothers? That is impossible to imagine of course. I hate to think what my own life would have been without my mother's patient care. It was at her knee that I learned to rely on faith. She was responsible for teaching me that through hard work everything is possible. She has always been there through victories and defeats. When a reporter asked me how I could explain my rapid rise in government to the position of advisor to the President of the United States, he looked surprised when I told him I owed it to my parents—particularly the influence of my mother.

Countless times each day a mother does what no one else can do quite as well. She wipes away a tear, whispers a word of hope, eases a child's fear. She teaches, ministers, loves, and nurtures the next generation of citizens. And she challenges and cajoles her kids to do their best and be the best. But no editorials praise these accomplishments—where is the coverage our mothers rightfully deserve?

Newspaper headlines about the disasters of drugs, suicide, and violence tell us loud and clear just how badly our young people need mothering. But it is the business pages of our newspapers which make great fanfare over the fact that "Ms. Jones is named the first female Vice President of Trendy, Cash and Now." The is the important news of the day!

There are no news stories telling us that today a child was taught what it means to be loved, an infant was hugged securely, or that the wonders of the classics were introduced to a young mind. No one seems to care that a house was made a home, or that a simple table of food was transformed into a place of community and nurturing.

In the trench wars of Washington, politicians fulminate about issues grand and small, many posturing themselves as friends of the family. But few of them understand how important the acts of love within the family really are. Few understand what a terrible fate awaits a society in which no one has time to offer those open arms that comfort a child. Even fewer take the time to stand up and praise the noble and generally thankless tasks that America's mothers perform each day.

What should we do while we wait for society to get its priorities straight? Speaking as a husband, I believe there is much that married men can do in their own homes. First of all, men, tell your wife you love her. Thank her for being in your home with your children. Let her know that the choices she has made are honored by you. In short, tell her how much she matters!

A 1985 study indicates that men fall far short in this important area. A majority of women indicated they have not received adequate emotional support from their husbands. Many women complained that their husbands didn't value "mothering." Others pushed their wives back into the work force even though the women preferred to be home with their children.

But it isn't too late to restore the fine art of motherhood back to its time-honored position in our society. In spite of the current cultural hostility, lack of support from husbands, and incredible pressures inside and outside the home, women continue to affirm the importance of motherhood.

A Roper poll published in *Ladies Home Journal* in 1988 reported on a survey of women who were asked to describe the best thing about being a woman today. Sixty percent said it is "motherhood." Being a wife was in second place, and the great achievement of feminism, "Taking advantage of women's increased opportunities," came in a distant fourth.[8]

At least, today's pervasive propaganda against bearing and raising children hasn't convinced everyone!

Flight from Fatherhood

It will not be enough for us to encourage mothers, however, if we do not also restore the role of fathers in the family as well. Study after study confirms that children have the best chance of success when both parents are present. Fatherhood must be re-emphasized not only for the sake of the family but for the sake of men. Here, too, the anti-traditional forces have promoted a philosophy that undercuts fidelity, promotes singleness, and entices men away from a commitment to hearth and home.

A man or woman faced with the temptation to cheat can find plenty of support for making an unwise decision in the popular culture. *Parade* magazine, for example, recently ran a front page story by Dr. Joyce Brothers on adultery. Brothers argues that infidelity can actually strengthen a marriage and she cites increasing infidelity by wives as a sign of the new equality between men and women.[9]

Larger research samples leave no doubt that the levels of infidelity are much lower than those cited by Joyce Brothers. But her article, and scores of others like it read by millions of people, have an impact. They help tempt both women and men away from the lifetime commitments they made—usually with disastrous results. And they make faithful men and women feel out of step and behind the times.

David Blankenhorn of the Institute for American Values has pointed out that the phrase "good family man" has almost disappeared from our popular language. This complement was once widely heard in our culture

—bestowed, to those deserving it, as a badge of honor. Rough translation: "He puts his family first." Ponder the three words: "good" (moral values); "family" (purposes larger than the self); and man (a norm of masculinity). Yet today within elite culture, the phrase sounds antiquated, almost embarrassing . . . contemporary American culture simply no longer celebrates, among its various and competing norms of masculinity, a widely shared and compelling ideal of the man who puts his family first.[10]

William Bennett put it succinctly in a 1986 speech on the family in Chicago when he asked, "Where are the fathers? . . . Generally, the mothers are there struggling. For nine out of ten children in single parent homes, the father is the one who isn't there. One-fifth of all American children live in homes without fathers. . . . Where are the fathers? Where are the men? Wherever they are, this much is clear: too many are not with their children."[11]

Nowhere is the flight from fatherhood more apparent than in the inner cities of our nation. There the full effect of the anti-family, "liberation" philosophy is painfully apparent. Much of the promise of the civil rights movement of the '60s and '70s has been destroyed by the break-up of the Black family. A Black child is now more than three times as likely as a White child to live in a father-less home.

Men enticed by drugs, easy sex, and the other temptations of urban life have abandoned the responsibility of parenting and husbanding. These bad choices have been made more likely by a culture that mocks traditional values and by government policies that many times discourage family formation.

Our current welfare system, for example, encourages the formation of "the mother-state-child family." Uncle Sam has become a marriage partner and "father" of last resort. The results are predictable—no bureaucrat, however well meaning, can substitute for a father.

Studies show that the absence of the father expresses itself in male children in two very different ways: it is linked to increased aggressiveness on one hand, and greater manifestations of effeminacy on the other. A 1987 study of violent rapists found that 60 percent of them came from single-parent homes. A Michigan State University study of adolescents who committed homicides found that 75 percent of them were from broken homes.[12] Girls without fathers fare no better. They become sexually active sooner and are more likely to have out-of-wedlock children.

But studies aren't necessary to discover what common sense tells us—intact families are better off—mothers and fathers both need to be there. Children need their parents. Too many of America's children are suffering from a "parent deficit."

Unbelievably, the truth of these statements is resolutely denied by the anti-tradition cultural army and its allies. The influence of feminism on the cultural elite is so strong that many in government and the media are unwilling to say clearly that, on the average, female-headed households are in great danger—particularly in the inner city with its many social problems.

The Penalty of Permissiveness

Just blocks from my office in downtown Washington, thousands of broken families are trying valiantly to claw their way out of the ghetto. Countless women try to raise out-of-wedlock babies abandoned by the men who took their pleasure and then joined the culture of the street where a fortune in drug profits or a quick bullet in the head are very real possibilities on any given weekend.

On many inner-city street corners, gangs of taunting teenage thugs harass women and children. They are products of a society where intact families are now the exception. The glib chatter of amateur sociologists on TV talk shows, the research papers of liberal academics, the social engineering of liberal judges, and the legislating of government bureaucrats have all sown seeds that have now grown into a twisted harvest of broken lives and crushed spirits. But with all the evidence stacked against the social experiments of the past three decades, the liberal elites are still singing their siren song of "liberation."

Toni Morrison, the Pulitzer Prize-winning Black author, was asked in a *Time* magazine interview about the
"worsening circumstances and statistics" of inner-city life,
including single-parent households and unwed teenage
pregnancies. She replied,

> Well, neither of those things seems to me a debility. I don't
> think a female running a house is a problem, a broken fam-
> ily. It's perceived as one because of the notion that a head is
> a man.
>
> Two parents can't raise a child any more than one. You
> need a whole community—everybody—to raise a child.
> The notion that the head is the one who brings in the most
> money is a patriarchal notion, that a woman—and I have
> raised two children, alone—is somehow lesser than a male
> head. Or that I am incomplete without the male. This is not
> true. And the little nuclear family is a paradigm that just
> doesn't work. It doesn't work for White people or for Black
> people. Why we are hanging onto it, I don't know. It isolates
> people into little units—people need a larger unit.[13]

Toni Morrison is wrong. It is possible, of course, to
raise a family without a father. Countless women struggle
against the odds and many do an incredible job. But it is
deceitful to suggest that on average a single mother can do
as well as an intact family. Such homes start out with the
odds against them. While courage, perseverance, and faith
can overcome those odds, it is preferable, for families and
for the future of our nation, that our children be raised in
homes with both parents.

We need to restore fatherhood to its rightful place of
honor. To the middle-class father we can praise his commitment to the economic well-being of his family, but we also
must remind him that more than a pay check is needed. His
loving leadership and partnership with his wife in the care
and nurture of children must be affirmed.

Fathers must be there to tame adolescent boys, to give
a young son a sense of what it means to be a man, and to

explain why honor and loyalty and fidelity are important. For daughters, a father is a source of love and comfort that can help her avoid surrendering her virtue in a fruitless search for love through premarital sex.

In the inner city, we must reinforce the place of men in the home. Welfare programs should stop replacing fathers. Tougher laws and a new seriousness about values must be pursued to remove the temptation of drugs and sex for sale in our cities. To all men a clear message must be sent: "you are needed in the home, now, standing with your wife in the important task of raising children and meeting your responsibility."

Changes in the popular culture could help too. The single man in our society is often portrayed as having the best of all worlds. Free access to numerous women, unburdened by responsibility, debts, and demands on his time. A host of lurid magazines present this enticing image of life without commitment.

But the facts tell another story. If women and children have suffered from the abandonment of men—men have also suffered from the consequences of their own flight from love and family.

Without a recommitment of fathers to the home, the cultural war over family and children will be won by those who believe that all lifestyles are equal. Those who believe that the State must be the ultimate parent will inevitably take charge of the family. Such an outcome will result in suffering for millions: men, women, and children alike. It will most certainly lead to the eventual collapse of America as a free democratic society.

We simply must stop that scenario here and now. This is where the civil war begins and where the cultural nightmare ends. From today on, we are at war!

Gary L. Bauer

10

FREEDOM
OR SLAVERY?

> If we fail to instruct our children in justice, religion, and liberty, we will be condemning them to a world without virtue, a life in the twilight of a civilization where the great truths have been forgotten.
>
> Ronald Reagan[1]

Close your eyes for a moment and try to picture the following imagery. A new nation wins its independence based on the revolutionary view that men have God-given rights, regardless of race, color or creed. This infant country grows and prospers in the years that follow bringing more wealth and opportunity to more people than any nation in the history of man.

Imagine further, that twice in one century, this nation would help save the world from tyranny by sending millions of its sons to fight and die in far off lands. Then, even though victorious, it neither occupied nor expanded its territory, but instead, spent billions of dollars to rebuild the ruined cities of its enemies and turned them into economic superpowers.

Imagine this country with a rich tradition, filled with heroes, known for its selflessness and generosity almost to a fault. Finally, imagine that a strange case of collective amnesia gripped these people, causing them to forget their own heritage and fail to transmit that rich tapestry of their history to their own children.

This scenario of a great nation that forgets its past has actually happened in the United States. For at least three decades, the heroic traditions of Western civilization have been stripped from our educational system's art, literature, and the culture. As a result, the children of the greatest experiment in history often graduate from our schools ignorant of the great men and women upon whose shoulders our civilization rests.

Aliens in Their Own Land

Driving home from work one day, I paused at a stoplight. To my right, a group of high school students sprawled on a lawn. A portable CD player blared heavy metal rock music.

The teens lay in the grass with their heads bopping to the beat of the music. They didn't appear to have a care in the world. One young man was smoking pot. The others were harassing pedestrians who walked by. Their blank stares and designer jeans reminded me of a quip I heard about some young people: "They have Calvin Kleins on their behinds and nothing in their minds."

I wondered if any of the kids had noticed a historical marker a few feet behind them. The plaque designated the site of a Civil War skirmish. The Washington area is peppered with such markers, but all too often the only people who stop and notice are tourists.

Yet, right on that spot, hundreds of men had paid the ultimate price for a great cause: liberty, freedom, and the preservation of a nation. Many who died were young boys, some even younger than the youths who whiled away the day listening to rock music.

What did these teens know about Bull Run, Antietam, or Fort Sumter? Did any of them understand what Abraham Lincoln meant by "patriot graves" bound together by "mystic cords of memory"? I hope they knew about this rich heritage.

I felt no anger at these kids lying there on the lawn. The blame for their ignorance of our history rests squarely on the shoulders of their parents and teachers, many of whom pass this place daily on the way to work or to shop. Had any of them pointed out the significance of that hallowed place to their children? Probably not. We live in an age that is uninformed of the past and unworried about tomorrow. The stresses of daily living are about all they can handle.

Roots That Sustain Us

Parents and children who don't feel any particular reverence at such places are reflecting the transparent values of our culture. That culture seems to elevate commerce and instant gratification above anything else.

As Washington and its suburbs continue to grow, the land is confiscated for shopping centers and freeways. Who cares whether our great-great-grandfathers fought an epic battle on this site? Who thinks twice about what this country would be like if we had lost the War for Independence or failed to resist tyranny in this century?

Perhaps your own town has witnessed zoning battles over historic lands. In recent years, I've seen battlefields at places like Manassas and Brandy Station get plowed under to make way for shopping centers and fast-food outlets.

When we cut ourselves and our children off from our roots and the heroes who sustained us, we guarantee that future generations will be deprived as well.

Unlike the hippies of the '60s, the teenagers I saw on the lawn that day had not rejected the American experience. More likely, no one had *taught* it to them. Since our culture has shirked its responsibility of teaching history and love of country to the young, our teenagers are adrift.

Still, loving one's country is a natural emotion—one that America's cultural elites constantly underestimate. Many of our sons and daughters feel it instinctively.

Some feel it because they've experienced sacrifice, too. Each year, on appropriate days, a Washington-area group called "No Greater Love" (made up of sons and daughters of those who died in service to their country) gathers in Arlington National Cemetery. They painstakingly decorate each grave site with a flower of remembrance.

When my oldest daughter was in the sixth grade, she entered an essay contest on what Memorial Day meant to her. Many essays poured in. The young writers talked about the beginning of summer and the end of school, but few mentioned the real meaning of the day.

My heart nearly burst with pride when Elyse was named the first place winner. Perhaps she won because of what we've taught her at home, or perhaps it was because just a month before, she had been in a Veterans hospital to visit my father, who has since passed away. This is what she wrote:

> When most people think of Memorial Day they think of parades, games and fun. During all of the excitement not many people think about what Memorial Day really means.
>
> Many men and women have died for our country to make sure that the generations after them can live in freedom. Memorial Day celebrates the freedom they gave us when they risked their lives for our country.

I was reminded of this once again when I visited my grandparents over Spring Break. My grandfather fought in World War II. During the War he was shot in the leg, causing him to have poor circulation. Later on it had to be amputated. He is now in a Veterans' Home and gets around in a wheelchair.

After taking my grandfather home and spending a few days with him we took him back to the Home. We stayed there for a while because we wanted to talk before leaving to go. When I was there I saw men who had sacrificed their arms, legs, sight and hearing. Some were unsure of who they are and who is President.

The children in my generation have not experienced a war. They have not had to say the scary good-bye to their older brothers or fathers as they march off to war. I hope we will not have to go through that scary time again, but if so I hope that this generation is as willing to die for their country and its freedom as my grandfather.

In these few simple lines my daughter showed that she understood a lot about sacrifice and devotion. But too many of our children have not been given the intellectual framework to defend their nation, nor an understanding of family, faith and freedom. In a world with competing ideologies, we send them intellectually disarmed into the fray. We cannot feign surprise when they lose.

Some Startling Facts

How far we have gone toward losing a common culture was made starkly clear by a national survey conducted in 1986 of over 8,000 students 17 years of age. The poll was funded by the National Endowment for the Humanities and was conducted by the National Assessment of Educational Progress (NAEP).[2]

On the history portion of the exam, the average student correctly answered 54.5 percent of the questions.

They fared worse on the literature portion: 52 percent. In other words, most of these teenagers "flunked out" when questioned about the history and literature of our civilization.

Specific questions were even more troubling. For example, when the 17-year-olds were given the key passage of the Declaration of Independence, "We hold these truths to be self-evident, that all men are created equal, that they are endowed by their Creator with certain unalienable Rights, that among these are Life, Liberty and the pursuit of happiness," fully one-third of them could not identify where the quote was from.

Less than half these adolescents knew that Lincoln said, "with malice toward none, with charity for all." Questions about recent history fared no better. Barely half knew that John F. Kennedy said, "And so, my fellow Americans, ask not what your country can do for you; ask what you can do for your country." And while 88 percent knew Martin Luther King said, "I have a dream," less than 60 percent knew that Franklin D. Roosevelt said of Pearl Harbor that it was "a day which will live in infamy."

One third of those tested did not know that the Declaration of Independence was signed between 1750 and 1800; two thirds could not place the Civil War within the period 1850-1900; nearly one half could not say within 50 years when World War I took place.

If you're still not shocked, less than 50 percent of our 16 and 17 year-olds recognized the names of Winston Churchill and Joseph Stalin! Another study showed that more of our children knew who Freddie Krueger was (of the gruesome *Nightmare on Elm Street* movies) than could correctly identify Abraham Lincoln.

In the literature section, students were asked, among other things, a variety of questions about the Bible *as literature*. This was not a test of religious belief but rather represented an effort to discover how much students knew about specific references in the Old and New Testaments that have influenced our culture and literature.

From Shakespeare to many contemporary literary works, it's impossible to understand what the author means without a knowledge of stories and phrases from the Bible. Large percentages of students—over 90 percent —recognized stories about Moses and Noah, proving that some core body of religious knowledge is still being passed on. But less than 60 percent knew the story of the Prodigal Son, and only 37.2 percent could identify the patience of Job. Nearly 40 percent could not say that King Solomon was known for his wisdom. Thirty percent didn't know Jesus was betrayed by Judas.

The response to one question from the original study, cited above, serves as a commentary on our times: only one-third of 17 year-olds knew the significance of Sodom and Gomorrah! No doubt the idea of cities or nations being destroyed because of immoral conduct must seem odd to the young, particularly if they have no knowledge of such a catastrophe happening in the past.

What's Going On?

From our literature, to our common history, to the struggle between freedom and slavery, our children don't seem to know the basic facts. Naturally, we should ask what content is emphasized in the school day if it is not this core curriculum of history and culture?

In many classrooms, precious time is spent on electives such as "teen living." In other cases fads have taken over. In the name of international understanding, children in some schools get heavy exposure to the culture of other nations before they are given a solid grounding in their own traditions. Precious little time is spent on American history. The history that *is* taught is most likely to be driven by political pressures.

Parents must not underestimate just how this educational process has deteriorated. A Task Force on Minorities in New York City has demanded all textbooks, even in science and math, be rewritten to reflect the contributions of various ethnic groups. The first line of the report explains the driving ideology of the authors. Clearly they hate America. They write:

> African Americans, Asian Americans, Puerto Ricans/Latinos and Native Americans have all been victims of an intellectual and educational oppression that has characterized the culture and institutions of the United States.[3]

A resource guide issued by the New York City Board of Education goes even further. Masculine terms like "forefathers" are to be eliminated from the school vocabulary. Males in pictures are not to be depicted as larger than females.[4] This is foolishness and represents the politicization of the classroom. Nothing is more likely to undermine citizen support for public education. Children shouldn't be pawns in some political game.

Some schools devote an entire month to Black history, while passing reference is made to the founding fathers. Let us be clear on this point. All children, Black and White, should know about such Black leaders as Martin Luther King, Crispus Attucks, and George Washington Carver. Our Black citizens have made a rich contribution to American life that was ignored for too long in our textbooks. Students need to know about the terrible injustice of slavery. But they also need to understand that White *and* Black Americans fought together to end it.

All our children should also be taught about Thomas Jefferson, James Madison, George Washington, Robert E. Lee, and Abraham Lincoln. Too many American textbooks no longer include the stirring quotes of our heroes and heroines, regardless of their race.

Our children are fed pap, watered down sentences, devoid of inspirational content. There has been a remarkable "dumbing down" of textbooks with the startling results that many of the books used by our sons and daughters are not even as challenging as the ones we studied 30 years ago. This trend must stop.

Abraham Lincoln said the philosophy of the classroom today will soon be the philosophy of the government tomorrow. He saw clearly the linkage between children and the direction the nation was moving.

Adolph Hitler agreed. He said, "Let me control the textbooks and I will control Germany." This critical nature of education is what makes today's crisis in the schools so ominous for the future.

If our children don't learn about the beliefs of the extraordinary men and women responsible for the creation and preservation of the American Republic, it will be impossible for them to understand or appreciate their legacy. And if they haven't been taught about the long list of tyrants who have enslaved and murdered millions, they will not be able to comprehend the continuing struggle today between freedom and slavery.

What a paradox it was to watch students in Tiananmen Square in China stand before a massive military force and quote the words of our founding documents before the TV cameras. One large poster written in English quoted Patrick Henry, "Give me liberty or give me death."

The young Chinese, longing for freedom, knew these historic Western quotes better than many of our own children today, and they certainly had a clearer understanding of free and totalitarian societies. Some teachers in 1990 expressed surprise that their students seemed uninterested in the collapse of communist governments in Eastern Europe. But, if a child does not understand why there was a Berlin Wall, he certainly will not comprehend the elation of the people when it is torn down.

A few years ago, a substitute teacher wrote in the *Washington Post* about the depressing experience he had while teaching three advanced government classes in a suburban Virginia school. He decided to poll his students on the basic question of whether the American system of government was morally superior to that of the Soviet Union? Fifty-one of the 53 high school seniors he asked— the brightest high school seniors in one of the best school systems in the country—saw no difference between the two.

These children could not morally distinguish between their own nation built on the basis of each individual having God-given rights, and another nation that has operated for over 70 years on the assumption that man is a mere creature of the state. Not coincidentally, the two children who did comprehend a difference were Vietnamese boat children. They had received a valuable education in reality when they experienced the collapse of their homeland into the darkness of totalitarianism.

How About Higher Education?

We can always hope that what our children miss in their first twelve years of schooling, they will pick up later as they attend our colleges and universities. Millions of parents spend billions of dollars to send their sons and daughters to institutions of higher learning in order to learn the great truths about freedom, faith, virtue, and liberty.

Unfortunately, on many university campuses the failure to teach about liberty and our common culture has also reached crisis dimensions. The most prestigious schools in the country used to lead the way—Harvard, Yale, Princeton—in passing on a core curriculum to our most educated youth. But it was precisely these universities that found themselves on the front line of America's cultural civil war in the '60s and '70s.

The line didn't hold. Faced with an attack by student radicals, liberal faculty members in many cases simply surrendered. Campus rules were changed, drug use winked at. Universities abrogated their responsibility to insist on standards of behavior.

The core curriculum itself died from a thousand slashes. Courses built on political agendas, from feminism to Black power, began to replace the classics. Curiously, the finest universities and colleges in the country seemed to be the first to break under the onslaught.

By the mid-1970s, the curriculum at Harvard was so fragmented that a special faculty committee was convened to develop a new core curriculum. Their report issued in May of 1978 contained this astonishing statement: "We do not think there is a single set of great books every educated person must master." That is an extraordinary statement. It means in practice that our intellectual class does not understand the need for a nation, particularly a free nation, to have a common culture.

According to Lynne Cheney, Chairman of the National Endowment for the Humanities, education requirements are so loosely structured that it is possible to graduate from 78 percent of the nation's colleges and universities without ever taking a course in the history of Western civilization!

The results are predictable. A 1989 study of U.S. college seniors showed that half of the students never heard of *Moby Dick* or *David Copperfield*. Half couldn't identify the Magna Carta or the Emancipation Proclamation. One quarter of our "best and brightest" thought the American Constitution contained the phrase, "From each according to his ability, to each according to his need," which was actually written by Karl Marx.[5]

In the place of a core curriculum there is an "elective system" that permits a student to graduate without having studied Plato, Shakespeare, the Bible, or the Federalist Papers.

And what menu of subjects replaces this core curriculum? Many students instead take courses in popular culture, such as Music 2, "Rock and Roll is Here to Stay" at Brown University, or interdisciplinary courses in sexuality, such as the one led by a classics professor at Kenyon College that focuses exclusively on homosexuality.

These courses are a mockery of the word "education." They don't elevate our young people. They provide them with no intellectual support for liberty. They don't arm them for the great debate of whether man is a mere creature of the state or whether he is as our founders believed, a creature of God endowed with certain rights.

This type of curriculum teaches that these issues are not even important—or certainly no more important than whether rock and roll is here to stay. They make a mockery of the notion that there is a common culture that is needed to hold a free nation together.

It is ironic that those enjoying the greatest freedom, including professors, often seem to display a principled ingratitude toward the basic values of American society. On too many campuses of our finest schools, the best and brightest students are taught to disdain the common rituals and beliefs of the American people.

Professors, whose salaries are paid by the taxes and tuition subsidies of millions of hard-working Americans, ridicule capitalism, attack family values, and rewrite American history, so that if it is taught at all, America is always the villain. Marxism may be dying as a philosophy in Eastern Europe, and even in the Soviet Union, but it is alive and well in many faculty centers in our universities.

In fact, the university faculties of our country are far to the left of the students they educate. A survey by the Carnegie Foundation for the Advancement of Teaching and the American Council of Education showed that, in 1989, 25 percent of university professors described themselves as leftist, 32 percent liberal, 16 percent middle of the road, 21 percent moderately conservative and 6 percent strongly conservative. At the same time only 9 percent of college freshmen considered themselves far left, 22 percent liberal, 56 percent middle of the road, 21 percent conservative and less than 2 percent far right.[6]

While this process took complete hold in the last 20 years, its roots can be seen many years earlier. The journalist and social commentator, Walter Lippman, delivered an insightful speech in 1940 entitled, *Education versus Western Civilization*. In it he outlined the trends he already saw developing in the universities in the free nations of the world. His observations ring even more true today. Lippman wrote,

> Modern education (however) is based on a denial that it is necessary or useful or desirable for the schools and colleges to continue to transmit from generation to generation the religious and classical culture of the Western World. It is, therefore, much easier to say what modern education rejects than to find out what modern education teaches.
>
> Modern education rejects and excludes from the curriculum of necessary studies the whole religious tradition of the West. It abandons and neglects as no longer necessary the study of the whole classical heritage of the great works of great men.

Fortunately, the democracies in the dark days of World War II were able to call on enough of our heritage and culture to resist the totalitarians marching across the globe, bent on conquest.

But If Not . . .

George Will reminded us a number of years ago of an incredible story that took place during the darkest days of World War II. In 1940, trapped on the beaches of Dunkirk, France, hundreds of thousands of British and French soldiers were near the point of surrender or certain death as Hitler's troops tightened the noose around them.

As the battle raged, one British officer was able to send a message back to London. He chose three simple words, "But if not. . . ." Will writes that the message "was instantly recognized as a quotation from the book of Daniel, where Nebuchadnezzar commands Shadrach, Meshach, and Abednego to worship the golden image or be thrust into the fiery furnace."

The three biblical heroes answer defiantly, ". . . our God who we serve is able to deliver us from the burning fiery furnace, and he will deliver us out of thine hand, O king. *But if not,* be it known unto thee, O king, that we will not serve thy gods, nor worship the golden image."

The message from Dunkirk was a pledge from the entrapped soldiers that they had faith in being rescued, *but if not* they would not cooperate, even at the price of death, with the evil conquerors of Europe. As such, the message was remarkable for its courage. But that the three words' significance was immediately understood "is stirring evidence of a community deriving cohesion from a common culture." Will concludes, "Today many universities do little to equip rising generations with a sense of being legatees of a shared and valuable civilization."[7]

What the ultimate outcome of this failure will be is hard to predict with certainty. But we have already seen a short-term result that should lead all of us to demand a rededication to teaching about liberty and its opponents.

Americans have been shocked to witness one spy scandal after another breaking into the morning headlines. The damage to our national security is bad enough, but just as disturbing is the motivation of the traitors. In the '30s and '40s, most spies were motivated by ideology. Today our most valuable secrets have been compromised—for money!

We shouldn't be surprised. If we are teaching that all cultures are relative—each as good as the other—why not make a few quick dollars selling out your nation? A man can only be a traitor to something specific—a set of values, or beliefs or philosophy. If there is nothing different, unique, or superior in the American experiment, why not make a few million dollars passing on pieces of paper to another culture that is no worse, no better than our own?

Few issues should be higher on the national agenda. We must make a national commitment to transmitting to the young our rich cultural, political, religious, and social heritage. We must stop producing strangers in their own land.

This can be done in a number of ways, particularly by looking at our own experience of passing on our heritage. Through a good bit of our history, including much of this century, there was a broad consensus that teaching our children citizenship, love of country and our common heritage was a central part of the educational enterprise.

Just how broad this consensus was can be shocking in view of the battle lines drawn in many schools today. In recent years, the National Education Association (NEA) has been in the forefront of liberal groups calling for more emphasis on international education, peace studies, and less emphasis on traditional citizenship courses.

At a recent convention, the NEA passed resolutions on everything from the need for homosexual counselors in our high schools to foreign policy issues. But in 1941, the NEA was quite a different group. Then it published a document called *The American Citizens Handbook* that showed a much better understanding of the obligation of free people to pass on their heritage to their children.

Consider, for example, one section of the handbook entitled "What the Flag Means." There one finds an essay by a former Supreme Court Chief Justice who writes,

> It means that you cannot be saved by the valor and devotion of your ancestors; that to each generation comes its patriotic

duty; and that upon your willingness to sacrifice and endure as those before you have sacrificed and endured rests the national hope.

It speaks of equal rights; of the inspiration of free institutions exemplified and vindicated; of liberty under law intelligently conceived and impartially administered. . . . It is eloquent of our common destiny.

Other sections of the *Handbook* affirm the religious foundation of our nation. In a section entitled, "Religious Ideals, the Foundation," we read,

The American concept of democracy in government had its roots in religious belief. The ideal of the brotherhood of man roots down into the fundamentals of religion. The teachings of the Hebrew Prophets of Jesus Christ inculcate the idea of brotherhood. The growth of the idea gave us the concept of democracy in government. It ennobled home life. It emphasized the sacredness of human personality.

Other sections of the *Handbook* dealt with patriotism, reliable standards of rights and wrongs, character building: in short, all of the things we seem to be so confused about in America today.

Former Secretary of Education William Bennett had a copy of the handbook brought to his attention in 1986 when I was serving with him at the Department of Education. We quickly realized the handbook represented a great opportunity to stimulate debate on the purposes of education in a free society.

In a speech before the National Association of Secondary School Principals, Bennett outlined the Handbook in great detail, praised the NEA's earlier wisdom and then issued a simple challenge for them to reissue it or to republish excerpts if they preferred. He even offered money from the federal government to help pay the costs of the new edition!

Unfortunately, we never heard from the union and quite frankly didn't expect we would. We knew their leadership in Washington had for a long time cast its lot with those in America's culture war who claim there is no core heritage to pass on to our children about citizenship or anything else. Apparently in 1941—perhaps because the world was racked with war—there was no such confusion.

Restoring Educational Traditions

Our schools must make a national commitment to teaching our traditions first. Then, and only then, will our children be able to appreciate the "internationalism" which is the latest fad in our public schools. American history must be a staple for all of our children—rich and poor and White and Black. We are not speaking here of history that portrays America as flawless and perfect. Nor do we mean a history that portrays America as an evil force that has given the world only misery.

If our textbook publishers can't publish, and our teachers can't teach a history that explains to our children the facts with an appropriate emphasis on our successes and our shortcomings, then they should step aside and make room for others who can.

We are convinced that if our children are given the facts, they will be both proud of their heritage and mindful of the great contribution their nation has made to human liberty. They will also recognize that America is an unfinished experiment and that our best days lie ahead. And finally, they will come to embrace the quiet patriotism that is born from knowing that in a world of killing fields and dictators, they have much of which to be proud.

One of the most tragic events during the Reagan Presidency was the Sunday morning terrorist bombing of the Marine barracks in Beirut, in which hundreds of

Americans were killed or wounded as they slept. Many of us can still recall the terrible scenes as the dazed survivors worked to dig out their trapped brothers from beneath the rubble.

A few days after the tragedy, I recall coming across an extraordinary story. Marine Corps Commandant Paul X Kelly, visited some of the wounded survivors then in a Frankfurt, Germany, hospital. Among them was Corporal Jeffrey Lee Nashton, severely wounded in the incident. Nashton had so many tubes running in and out of his body that a witness said he looked more like a machine than a man; yet he survived.

As Kelly neared him, Nashton, struggling to move and racked with pain, motioned for a piece of paper and a pen. He wrote a brief note and passed it back to the Commandant. On the slip of paper were but two words—*"Semper Fi"* the Latin motto of the Marines meaning "forever faithful."

With those two simple words Nashton spoke for the millions of Americans who have sacrificed body and limb and their lives for their country—those who have remained faithful.[8]

Faithful, to What?

Faithful to what? What motivates these men? Where do we get them? They don't die for the right to produce pornography. They don't put their lives on the line for the right to abort unborn children. They don't sacrifice for designer jeans or low marginal tax rates. The America that has inspired such selflessness has not been a country whose highest value was relativism or commercialism.

It has been a nation that believed in something—that believed some things deserved to be loved and honored; a country of strong families, of faith in its destiny, knowing its rights are God-given. Without these beliefs, a nation committed to nothing more than the accumulation of wealth and material pleasures will soon find that it has no Corporal Nashtons, no Horatio to stand at the bridge, and ultimately, no liberty.

Being faithful means we have an obligation to learn and teach our children the precise specialness of the American experiment. The famous historians, Will and Ariel Durant, have written,

> If a man is fortunate he will, before he dies, gather up as much as he can of his civilized heritage and transmit it to his children. And to his final breath he will be grateful for this inexhaustible legacy, knowing that it is our nourishing mother and our lasting life.[9]

We must oppose those who deny and denigrate the values that distinguish us from other nations. We must constantly reassert to our neighbors, to those who teach our children, to the pols and pundits that this nation, its government, history and heritage must be taught if we are going to survive and pass our liberties on to the next generation of young Americans.

As parents, you can take these immediate actions. Whether they are taught at your own local school or not, nothing prohibits you from introducing your children to the founding documents of our democracy. Read them the Declaration of Independence, Washington's Farewell Address, Lincoln's *Gettysburg Address*, Martin Luther King's "I Have a Dream" speech. By sharing these things we give our children a cause for allegiance. By acquainting them with the heritage of America and its basis in a universal truth— that "all men are created equal" we give them a sense of America's strength.

The words of our great men and women can serve us well in this effort. We urge each of you—go back to our history—take your children with you. This must be your call. Teach your children to love the things you love and to honor the things you honor—nothing less will do.

Gary L. Bauer

11

ART AS AN IDEOLOGICAL WEAPON

"Art must again touch our lives, our fears and cares. It must evoke our dreams and give hope to the darkness."
Frederick Hart
Washington Post 8/22/29

All of us hope that our children will be exposed to art and literature as part of their education. We want them to be familiar with the great paintings and artists and read the stirring poetry and literature that is part of our heritage. We even hope that eventually they will know what good music sounds like.

The arts have played a crucial role in civic life throughout history. In a world that is often made ugly through human error, the arts remind us of beauty; sometimes they also serve to bring us face to face with the unpleasant side of reality. Either way, the independent creativity of the artist generally serves the common good.

But not always. In recent years, the arts have become another battlefield in our civil war. And increasingly the art that prevails among the trend setters is nihilistic, debasing, blasphemous and disgusting. This art doesn't enlighten or inspire. It debases and depresses.

For years many Americans have averted their gaze from this art, choosing to ignore it. But in recent years, ideological artists have become more aggressive as they have attempted to foist on society their dark vision of life without meaning. As Representative Henry Hyde put it:

> America is . . . involved in a *kulturkampf* . . . a war between cultures and a war about the meaning of culture." This struggle is between those who embrace "classic Jewish and Christian morality" and "those who are determined that those norms will be replaced with a radical and thoroughgoing moral relativism.[1]

This is no exaggeration. Take the work of Andres Serrano. His contribution to our artistic life consisted of taking a crucifix, the symbol of Christianity understood around the world, and submerging it in a jar of his own urine. When outraged citizens protested, the same tired old charges of censorship were raised by the liberal establishment.

Following close on the heels of this example in free expression came the work of another "artist," Robert Mapplethorpe, who died of AIDS in 1988. His exhibit of photographs contained pictures that art critics genteelly described as "homoerotic." In fact, sandwiched between nondescript photos in the exhibit were pictures showing a man urinating into his lover's mouth as well as a self-portrait of the artist himself, doubled over, without pants, and with a bullwhip dangling from his rectum.

Another photo shows a man hanging upside down, nude, with his arms and legs chained while a second man fondles the nude man's genitals. Mixed with pictures of this degeneracy were photos showing prepubescent children with the camera carefully focused on their exposed genitalia.

Some defenders of the Mapplethorpe exhibit asserted with a straight face that a photo of a little girl, with her dress pulled up so that her vagina is exposed, was really a reference to the Greek myth of innocence in the world. That "educated" men and women would claim this, in an age with skyrocketing rates of child molestation and abuse, is incredible. Children in a civilized society must not be made the focus of sexual interest—not in the name of art, or by false appeals to sophistication; not for entertainment, not for any reason—ever.

As one critic noted, the Mapplethorpe exhibit contained the kind of pictures which are "more commonly known as child pornography, when they're not federally funded." Federally funded? There is the final insult. Both the Serrano work and the Mapplethorpe exhibit were paid for with tax revenues—the hard-earned money working men and women give to their government in good faith for the common good. The grants were issued by the National Endowment for the Arts (NEA) one of Washington's previously lesser known bureaucracies with a 1988 budget of $170 million.

Setting Priorities

In a time of budget stringency, there are many projects that cry for tax revenues—the homeless, the war on drugs, education, hunger, maintaining a strong defense, AIDS research. It is doubtful that many Americans would put government paid decadent art high on this list.

News of these federally funded works of trash brought a firestorm of criticism around the country. Outraged pro-family groups joined conservative members of Congress to demand a review of the NEA grant process. In an age of run-away budget deficits, why was government money being used to subsidize this sort of exhibitionism?

The controversy received the usual biased presentation in the major media. Commentators with furrowed brows shook their heads in disbelief at the blatant effort to censor the Mapplethorpe exhibit. Quickly, the chant "First Amendment, First Amendment" built to a crescendo. Not surprisingly during these learned discussions about what is true "art," the only photos shown to the TV audiences were the less provocative ones.

Even in this age when anything goes, no network producer was foolish enough to actually permit the pictures that caused the outrage to be shown on the air. Instead, average Americans were shown the more acceptable photos. In fact, a full page ad placed in the *Washington Post* to defend the Mapplethorpe exhibit showed a simple vase with a single flower under the headline "Are you going to let politics kill art?"

The message was clear—only philistines could object to this mainstream art. Meanwhile, newspapers that joined the chorus against censorship didn't hesitate to turn down ads by citizen groups showing the actual photos that were generating the controversy.

One Washington gallery concerned about the controversy canceled their scheduled exhibit of Mapplethorpe's works. The gallery director quickly learned the truth of an old Washington adage—"no good deed goes unpunished." Demonstrators from the artistic and homosexual communities surrounded the gallery in a noisy demonstration chanting "Shame, Shame." Using a high tech projector they flashed pictures of the Mapplethorpe exhibit on the walls of the offending gallery.

Another Washington gallery, seeing an opportunity in the controversy, immediately agreed to display the photographs. The exhibit opened to record crowds with more than 5,500 people visiting the gallery in the first three days. Clearly the cultural elite in Washington were using their feet to send the rest of us a message: "If you find the exhibit offensive that is reason enough for us to embrace it."

Eventually the Congress responded to growing constituent outrage and adopted an amendment that infuriated the art bureaucracy and its liberal allies. The amendment, introduced by Senator Jesse Helms, prohibited NEA support for art that contained, as it stated, obscene or indecent materials, "including but not limited to depictions of sado-masochism, homo-eroticism, the exploitation of children, or individuals engaged in sex acts; or material which denigrates the objects or beliefs of the adherents of a particular religion or non-religion; or material which denigrates, debases, or reviles a person, group, or class of citizens on the basis of race, creed, sex, handicap, age, or national origin."

As Senator Helms so articulately put it in an interview in the *New York Times*, "If someone wants to write ugly nasty things on the men's room wall, the taxpayers do not provide the crayons."[2]

The reaction of the art community and of some bureaucrats at the NEA was to thumb their nose at this duly passed law of the U.S. Congress. At the College Art Association's annual conference meeting in New York in February of 1990, artists and academics gathered and made it clear that they felt they had a right to produce anything they wanted *and* have it paid for by the American taxpayer.

Revisionist Rhetoric

One art historian—Mary-Margaret Goggin—drew parallels between the opposition to porn art to the era of Nazi Germany. An anthropologist at Columbia University's

School of Public Health referred to what she called "moral panic" that threatened the art world. One artist, Hans Haacke, made it clear the progressive art community was ready for a fight. "Artists and Art institutions have to learn how to play hardball," Haacke said. "A democratic society needs a democratic art (taxpayer funded) and we have a right to demand it."[3]

Soon other outrages came to public attention. New "artistic works" pictured Christ as a drug junkie injecting cocaine into his needle-ridden arm. One artist displayed a jar with fetal parts from her own abortion. In New York a porn artist did her usual act which included urinating on stage and inviting members of the audience to inspect her cervix with a flashlight. The theater in which she performed was the direct recipient of NEA money as well as subsidies from the New York State Art Commission.

As outrageous as these events were, they provided the average American a vivid glimpse of the battle raging over the control of culture—a battle being won by degenerates masquerading as artists. The winners must have taken great pleasure not only in their victory but in forcing middle class Americans whom they despise to subsidize their filth with hard-earned tax money.

These incidents were outrageous to millions of Americans, including many members of the art community. For the first time some Americans were seeing the true clash of values in our culture. A letter from members of Congress to the Acting Chairman of the NEA objecting to the exhibits referred to a "very clear and unambiguous line" separating art from rubbish. Most of us would agree there is such a line. It must have come as a shock to the Congressmen that the art world recognizes no such line.

In fact, the same relativism we have seen reflected in the schools and in other parts of our public life totally permeates the art world too. To the avant-garde artist, the fact that an average man may find a photograph or painting or sculpture repugnant or offensive is proof that the "art" has accomplished its purpose—to offend the sensibilities and ridicule the values and beliefs of those with a traditional point of view.

One of the speakers outside the Washington gallery that canceled the Mapplethorpe exhibit put it this way, "If art is to remain something other than a blue-chip commodity, it will challenge and offend, especially those whose power rests in the status quo."

Garrison Keillor, the bestselling author and radio personality, went a step further. He bemoaned the fact that the National Endowment for the Arts had apparently funded "only" 20 pieces of porn art. He stated,

> The endowment has made the mistake of embarrassing itself on 20 occasions, and I wish it could do so more often. I don't regard those 20 controversial pieces as errors. I wish there were more—30 or 50 at least. The lesser number is testimony to how timid and repressed the arts are.[4]

The whole point is that the art is purposely made offensive, obscene and provocative as a way to spit in the eye of those who honor and love different things. For the homosexual community, it provides a way of flaunting their agenda and desensitizing the public to deviant behavior.

But those who assault tradition go one step further. They are not content to be merely tolerated—they insist on being subsidized. They demand that we pay the bill while they ridicule the fabric of our value system, including family, faith, and freedom.

Earlier in 1988, Americans were treated to another spectacle, courtesy of the art world—this one offering a hint of what young artists are being taught. At the taxpayer supported Chicago School of Art, an exhibit was put on display that required the viewer to step on an American flag in order to view the "art."

There was, of course, no shortage of radical artists, malcontents, and political extremists all too ready to wipe their feet on a symbol for whom millions of men and women have bled and died. But, that was the whole point—to defame what most Americans hold dear. Then when criticism mounts, the "artists" use the trump card of American politics—the First Amendment to the Constitution—as their defense.

Nihilism on the March

Anyone who has spent time in urban America has seen another manifestation of this subsidized attack on form and beauty in the arts. From San Francisco to Washington D.C., the urban landscape is littered with stone monstrosities, giant girders, and tilted metal, all masquerading as art and foisted on the American people in the name of artistic freedom.

Each year the General Services Administration has been spending one half of one percent of its public buildings budget for sculptured works more suitable for the junk yard than the public square.

For example, Federal Plaza in downtown Manhattan was dominated for nearly eight years by "Tilted Arc," a 120 foot-long, 12 foot-high rusted-metal sculpture weighing six tons. Sculptor Richard Serra was commissioned by the government to create the sculpture for $181,000. It was finally removed after a series of lawsuits.

Another piece of government-funded art, in front of the Social Security Administration building in Chicago, attracted the attention of then Senator William Proxmire who gave it his Golden Fleece award for the project most representing government waste in 1982.

Nearly every city and state has had to put up with similar art intended to shock middle class and traditional sensibilities. Massachusetts artist Michael Thompson was allowed to place his work funded by the Massachusetts Artists Foundation in the atrium concourse of the State Transportation Building in Boylston. Thompson's work had a little more form than some of the other monstrosities—it consisted of a ring of toilets.

Seeing such curiosities, most of us are at first outraged and then we wonder what bureaucrat decided to do this to us. Then we are merely puzzled—what are we to make of these monuments to nihilism? Finally, we learn to tolerate, subconsciously accepting the whole point the artist and his government allies wanted to make—nothing is beautiful, or good, or has boundaries or form.

Obviously someone important—an artist, and some- one else (some government official)—thought this painting or sculpture to be profound and meaningful. Who am I, we wonder, to question it? It's all only a matter of taste.

Does it matter? In the grand scheme of things, how upset should ordinary people be about the extraordinary effrontery that masquerades as art? The answer is, very upset! When American churches, businesses, corporations, and other educational institutions surrender without protest to nihilist, relativist, secular-humanist art, we are surrendering on another battlefield in America's cultural civil war.

When Art Is True and Beautiful

Frederick E. Hart designed the beautiful bronze statue, the three servicemen, that stands near the Viet- nam War Memorial in honor of the thousands who gave their lives in that far off conflict. Hart is an artist. He knows the forces at work in the profession to which he has devoted his life. Hart believes,

> What is really going on is the cynical aggrandizement of art and artist at the expense of sacred public sentiments—

profound sentiments embodied by symbols, such as the flag, or the crucifix, which the public has a right and a duty to treasure and protect.

Hart reminds us of an example of ennobling art, not produced by some self-described artistic nihilist, but by a group of "artists" who probably paid with their lives for their work.

The most touching and noble impulse toward "visible speech" in recent times was the short-lived creation of the Statue of Democracy in Tiananmen Square. Naively executed, it was nonetheless a wonderful display of the unique ability of art to embody and enhance concisely and movingly a deeply felt public yearning for an ideal of a just society. The profound meaning the statue had for tens of millions of people gives the art a value and moral authority of profound significance.[5]

By the way, Hart himself, recognized as one of our country's best sculptors, could not get a grant from the National Endowment for the Arts for his work on the facade of the National Cathedral. "The NEA turned me down flat, basically because my work was representational and religious. Their opinion was, this is not art."

While Hart nearly starved to death after being rejected by the NEA, he persevered. His work at the National Cathedral, "The Creation Sculptures," including free standing figures of Adam and St. Peter, will be unveiled this summer. Presumably Hart would have had better luck getting federal funds if he would have only taken the additional step of suspending his work in a vat of urine or showing his figures engaged in sado-masochistic acts.

Art tells us much about what a people think about themselves and the world around them. This nation, any nation, absorbs values through its art. If the art is decadent, the people will be decadent; and the reverse is equally true.

Consider this description of the art of another nation at another time. The art:

> "totally rejected accepted aesthetic standards: The painters were fascinated by ugliness; the composers threw harmony overboard, gradually moving toward dissonance; the poets and playwrights were preoccupied with the madness of great cities, parenticide and rats emerging from rotten corpses." Beneath all of this was "the wish to shock a self satisfied, satiated world and the artists' enemies, which included the state, the middle classes, the philistines and authority in general."

This could easily be a description of America in the '80s and '90s, but in fact it is commentary from a book by Walter Laqueur about the pre-Hitler years in Germany.[6] This unrestrained decadence helped kill German democracy in its cradle and eventually contributed to the horrors of Nazism.

In Washington, D.C., one fortunately can still see the evidence of an earlier age when sculpture had form and meaning and monuments were built to honor something. From the majestic Lincoln memorial to the hundreds of other statues marking the contributions of great men in battle and service to their country, much of Washington is living witness to an age where public art reinforced the beliefs and traditions of a confident nation.

But slowly the formless new art encroaches. In the middle of the Hart Senate Office Building stands an Alexander Calder mobile of metal clouds and mountains weighing tons, paid for by you, and a monument to nothing other than the ability of nihilistic artists to feed at the public trough.

Currently being installed in front of the CIA headquarters in Langley, Virginia, is a $250,000 conglomeration of rocks and crystals that some see as a tribute to the New Age philosophy. In an earlier time the nation would have erected a sculpture representing the sacrifice of intelligence agents who have died in service to their country.

Nobility of Purpose

Plato wrote: "Seek artists whose instincts guide them to what is lovely and gracious so that our young men may drink in from noble works." Even if one concedes that beauty is in the eye of the beholder, certainly most of us would conclude that a photo of a man urinating into the mouth of another or, for that matter, 200 tons of formless rock dropped into a public square, doesn't qualify as beauty under any standard.

If we can't agree on the definition of art, then at least we *can* resolve that we will not allow ourselves to be forced to pay for artistic terrorism with the money earned by millions of hard-working Americans.

Of course, it is not only government that throws away our money on this trash. Corporations too, give millions of dollars in subsidy each year to the arts, and while much of it is well spent, too much of it goes to support the avant-garde. Ultimately democratic capitalism can only be preserved in a society that can draws lines—between right and wrong, good and bad, beautiful and ugly, meaningful and nihilistic.

It is only in a society whose culture reflects these distinctions that workers and consumers are capable of sustaining a free economy. There is something paradoxical about corporate chieftains siphoning off profits to subsidize art which undermines and ridicules every value which made the corporate profits possible in the first place.

Keeping Our Focus

What has all this got to do with our children? A lot. Our children are most at risk, since those fighting the cultural war against traditional values perceive our children as "the prize." The most troubling photo in the Mapplethorpe exhibit is of a disheveled young girl, perhaps five or six years old, sitting vulnerably alone on concrete steps. The "artist" has managed with his camera lens to look up her dress at her parted legs, thus turning all who visit the exhibit into voyeurs preying on this child's innocence.

But even when our children are not being so directly exploited, they are the ultimate target for the cultural message that all rules are prohibited, that everything is permissible, that nothing has value or goodness or deserves to be honored. It is the same message that all too many of our children receive in some school and university classrooms.

It is the same point reiterated in the heavy metal music and in comic books that no longer resemble the clean, innocent stories they represented in our own youth. The message being sent is that nothing is good or bad, decent or repugnant. Everything is the same and of equal value. All of it is to be tolerated and embraced in the name of liberty. But as St. Paul wrote in Philippians,

> whatsoever things are true, whatsoever things are honest, whatsoever things are just, whatsoever things are pure, whatsoever things are lovely, whatsoever things are of good report; if there be any virtue, and if there be praise, think on these things.

America is better than the fashionable artists and cultural elite would have us believe. It remains only for good and decent people to say "enough" and insist that those who represent us in Washington stop subsidizing decadence.

Gary L. Bauer

12
THAT'S
ENTERTAINMENT

The impact of television and movies in the battle over family and children has been profound. In the case of television, the impact has not only been the message it sends, but the effect it has had on family life.

In many homes, dinner conversation has been replaced by shared staring at "the tube." Time in the evening, once reserved for families to share their experiences of the day, is now replaced by television watching.

Researchers estimate that the average child between the ages of 6 and 18 will spend between 15,000 and 16,000 hours watching TV compared to 13,000 hours spent in school. Even children younger than 6 will have put in many hours of viewing—particularly in broken homes where the television becomes an electronic babysitter.

The implications are horrendous. In fact, if the statistics are true, by the time the average American youngster is six, he will spend more time watching TV than he will spend talking to his father in a lifetime.

George Gallup, Jr., President of the Gallup Poll, has suggested that,

> If more Americans could be persuaded to carve out of their three or four hours of television viewing each day a period of five minutes at bedtime and use this time to ask their child a simple question—"How did things go today?"—and *listen*, the results in terms of individual families and society as a whole could, I believe, be highly salutary.[1]

This is the minimum parents should do. Even better would be at least one evening a week reserved for family activities with the TV set off.

The number of hours children spend in front of the TV set is troubling. Of more concern is the anti-tradition, anti-family message that permeates so many programs as well as the constant diet of violence, and consequence-free, easy sex.

Numbing the Minds of the Young

By graduation day, the average high school student has seen 18,000 murders in 22,000 hours of television viewing. According to studies done at the Annenburg School of Communications in Philadelphia, 55 percent of prime-time characters are involved in violent confrontations once a week. In the real world, the world television pretends to portray, the figure wouldn't even be one percent.

Recently, significant government deregulation of the airwaves, along with network cutbacks of those divisions that monitor network standards, have caused the flood gates to open. Language that just a few years ago would have been prohibited is now broadcast into our living rooms during what used to be considered a family viewing time.

Scenes of incredible violence are commonplace during prime time. One made-for-TV movie not only depicted sexual bondage on the air but, in addition, viewers were treated to the scene of a dog licking up blood oozing from a murder victim's head.

Dr. Leonard D. Efrom, Professor of Psychology at the University of Illinois at Chicago, conducted a 22-year study of 400 TV viewers. He concluded,

> There can no longer be any doubt that heavy exposure to televised violence is one of the causes of aggressive behavior, crime and violence in society.

The American Academy of Pediatrics recently urged that children should watch no more than two hours of television a day, to limit damage caused by violence and sex-saturated programming.[2] But many in the TV industry feel they are in a crusade to constantly test the limits of permissible programming. Steve Bochco, the producer of NBC's popular "L.A. Law," has said,

> I would like to access the normal, casual profanity that you have in any walk of life. . . . I'm an equal opportunity offender. . . . If broadcast standards didn't exist, I'd be happy.

Parents are increasingly upset by what they see. A poll taken for the "Family Channel" showed that 58 percent of parents were "frequently" or "occasionally" uncomfortable with something they watched in a TV program with their children. Only 17 percent said they were "never" uncomfortable.

A poll for *Parents* magazine shows that a backlash is building as the discontent felt by the average parent increases. Two-thirds of those polled said there should be standards to prohibit some material from being shown. Some 74 percent want an end to vulgar, four-letter words on the airwaves; 72 percent feel the same about programs that ridicule and make fun of religion; and 64 percent want

TV networks to stop showing programs that ridicule traditional values, such as marriage or motherhood. Not surprisingly, over 70 percent of the respondents thought TV programming overall was mediocre to terrible.[3]

This discomfort is due in part to subtle messages that television programming sends as well as the overt violence and profanity. By and large, television programming reflects the anti-family side of America's cultural civil war. In fact, for years the intact family has been a TV oddity. There are noteworthy exceptions of course—"The Cosby Show" and the now-canceled "Family Ties," for example. But Tom Shales, the TV critic for the *Washington Post*, noticed the disappearing traditional family as he previewed the 1988-89 television season. Shales observed,

> Thematically, prime time is strictly splitsville. With the arguably glorious exception of ABC's "Roseanne," families are the focus of the new weekly shows only if the families are broken ones. Single parents, widows, widowers, and divorced husbands and wives have proliferated. To a TV programmer, just about the only marriage that works is the marriage that doesn't work. (*Washington Post* 10/2/88)

Shales isn't the only one to notice the curious trend. While TV producers knock down the old taboos in order to depict more nudity, kinky sex, and profanity, they seem to be self-censoring themselves in other areas. Television critic Jeff Greenfield has noted that prime-time television deals with every issue except those most fundamental to our being. He wrote,

> They have moved into areas once considered untouchable in prime time; yet the most common, most crucial area of all time—the capacity of modern men and women to love, trust, share, and provide a moral framework for children, this seems to be beyond their grasp.[4]

Clearly on both television and in the movies, religion is often either ignored, or worse, ridiculed and attacked. Dr. Martin Marty of the University of Chicago says that his examination of popular films shows that there is no doubt that religion is slighted in the movies. Marty says, "We baptize, circumcise, and marry in the name of it; if we face death, we call on it as the most profound resource. For Hollywood to so symptomatically screen out that dimension is strange."[5]

Unfortunately, the cultural elite and its values control the "high ground" in Hollywood. From that perch they are able to constantly promote the values they believe in—secularism, modernity, sexual liberation, radical feminism —and they denigrate the values they reject—religious faith, tradition, family, and patriotism. The values of Hollywood are, by and large, at war with the values of the average American.

While many television executives deny that they are influencing public thinking or attitudes, Ted Turner of Cable News Network can at least be credited with honesty. Speaking to a group of broadcasters from around the world, Turner made this surprising confession:

> Your delegates to the United Nations are not as important as the people in this room (broadcasters). We are the ones that determine what the people's attitudes are. It's in our hands. (*AFA Journal* October, 1989)

If Turner is right—what kind of hands are molding public opinion? Turner, himself, has said that "Christianity is a religion for losers." On another occasion he called Christians "bozos." He suggested recently that the wisdom of the Ten Commandments should be replaced by his own set of rules—including the idea that no family may have more than two children or no more than the government suggests. Unfortunately, Turner—while an arrogant odd-ball—is not alone in his alienation from traditional American values.

The Devaluation of Values

The comprehensive Rothman-Lichter survey of Hollywood attitudes shows a wide gap between the prevailing values there and in the mainstream of American life. Of the entertainment elite surveyed in Hollywood, only 33 percent were of the view that adultery is wrong, and only 5 percent said the same about homosexuality.

While the country seems split right down the middle on the abortion debate, fully 91 percent of Hollywood's elite favored abortion. Over 90 percent of entertainment personalities "seldom or never attend religious services."[6] In fact, Hollywood seems to be a center for more bizarre views in the faith realm with some referring to it as a "city of cults." It is hard to imagine a city more isolated from mainstream American views.

These television producers and Hollywood executives control a powerful medium. Their values inevitably are pushed on the rest of us. The renowned actor, Charlton Heston, is troubled by many of the trends in his business, and he realizes the power of the silver screen. In a recent interview he said,

> The moving image is the most powerful tool or weapon to change and shape the way people feel about the world and themselves. The printed word is almost primitive—like hammer and stone—measured against film and television. Its influence doesn't compare.[7]

Releasing the power of television, anti-traditional forces in our culture are planning on new ways to use it to reshape our attitudes and to win our children to a new world view. In a remarkably frank book called *After the*

Ball, two homosexual activists, Marshall Kirk and Hunter Madsen, have outlined their plan to promote the widespread acceptance of homosexuality through subtle changes in TV programs and paid advertising.

According to the authors:

> . . . the TV screen radiates its embracing bluish glow for more than 50 hours every week. . . . These hours are a *gateway* into the private world of straights, through which a *Trojan horse* might be passed.[8]

Of course the Trojan Horse is the idea that homosexuality is normal and acceptable. Each week TV sitcoms, talk shows and news reports are already promoting that idea.

James Hitchcock has pointed out that the entertainment industry constantly attacks traditional Americans. He writes,

> Such people are routinely depicted as insecure, stupid, neurotic, and ridiculous. In television fiction, for example, religion is often shown as a deforming influence, rarely as a positive and supportive element in people's lives. Religious believers are either hypocrites or fanatics.[9]

Sometimes Hollywood goes too far, dropping its subtle undermining of faith and family for a more overt attack that Americans clearly perceive as hostile to their beliefs. The controversy over *The Last Temptation of Christ* is one such example. The movie which portrayed Christ as a neurotic, sex-fantasizing, reluctant Savior caused a storm of protest and movie boycotts.

There is no question that under our system of Constitutional liberties, Universal Pictures *can* produce and show such a movie. They clearly are permitted to do so. The question is whether *they should have made* a film that insulted millions of God-fearing Americans and mocked their most deeply held beliefs.

The Unprotected Majority

It is impossible to imagine a film being produced in Hollywood that mocked Martin Luther King or Anne Frank, although the Constitution would permit it. Such a film would be inappropriate. Both individuals touch the deepest emotions of millions of Americans. Yet Hollywood thought it was fair game to debunk the life of a Man who is the central defining force in the lives of millions of individuals in every nation in the world.

While we are constantly warned to be "sensitive" in how we depict or talk about various ethnic and racial groups, apparently in Hollywood "Christian-bashing" is acceptable entertainment. In Hollywood, and much of the rest of our culture, only traditionalists can be defamed with impunity.

It wasn't always so, of course. Not that many years ago Hollywood routinely turned out biblical blockbusters —movies like *Ben Hur, The Ten Commandments,* or the *Greatest Story Ever Told.* Today's Hollywood is quite different.

Michael Medved who co-hosts the weekly PBS program "Sneak Previews" recently said that "Hostility toward traditional religion runs so deep and burns so intensely that filmmakers insist on expressing it even at the risk of commercial disaster." As an example he cited the movie, *King David,* starring Richard Gere, in which the king is portrayed as abandoning his religious "delusions" and rejecting God at the end of his life. This historical travesty cost $28 million and sold less than $3 million in tickets. But what's a few dollars if it advances your ideology?

Hollywood is a powerful weapon in our cultural civil war. It's values, in the guise of entertainment, are promoted in our living rooms and on thousands of movie screens. Our children are particularly influenced by the value messages they receive that ridicule traditional beliefs and undercut commitment to family and faith.

Rock Music

In addition to the influence of television, hard rock music and music videos also are playing a role in the undermining of family values. In addition, evidence is growing that links heavy metal music to a variety of youth dysfunctions, including drug abuse and premarital sex.

A special subcommittee of the American Medical Association reports that the average teenager listens to 10,500 hours of rock music between the 7th and 12th grades. These listening hours tend to be even less supervised than time spent in front of the TV. The Committee urged doctors to be alert to the listening habits of young patients as a clue to their emotional health.[10]

A number of popular rap groups routinely use racial slurs, depict women being raped, and promote anti-Semitism. Groups such as Ice-T, Axl Rose, Guns and Roses, as well as others, make millions of dollars appealing to our most debased instincts. Rap groups like N.W.A. and 2 Live Crew call for a war on police. Heavy-metal groups, including the Beastie Boys and Motley Crue, use satanic images and mimic masturbation on stage.

Tipper Gore, President of the Parents' Music Resource Center and wife of Senator Albert Gore, Jr., of Tennessee, has raised some alarming statistics.

In America, a woman is raped once every six minutes. A majority of children surveyed by a Rhode Island Rape Crisis Center thought rape was acceptable. In New York City, rape arrests of 13 year-old boys have increased 200 percent in the past two years. Children 18 and younger now are responsible for 70 percent of the hate crime committed in the United States. No one is saying this happens solely because of rap or rock music, but certainly kids are influenced by the glorification of violence.[11]

At the very least, record albums and videos should be subjected to the same kind of rating system that is currently used to help parents steer away from inappropriate movies. Radio stations should refrain from playing music that demeans our citizens on the basis of race and that encourages anti-female violence and exploitation.

There is little likelihood that Hollywood's worldview will change soon. Those fighting for traditional values will have to prepare themselves to face a hostile pop culture for years to come. But traditionalists are not powerless. Consumer boycotts of corporations that sponsor TV programming can be effective—particularly when those companies are marketing products that depend on a family market. Washington should be pressured to enforce standards against indecency on the public airways.

Several Republican Administrations have campaigned in favor of traditional values but then appointed members to the Federal Communications Commission who were more interested in deregulation than in safeguarding community standards on the public airways. However, currently the FCC is attempting to block indecent broadcasts 24 hours a day. It is a step in the right direction.

The Power of the Purse

The film industry also responds to consumer pressure. While press stories reported long lines at *The Last Temptation of Christ*, those lines were due to the opening of the movie in only one or two theaters in major cities. In fact, the makers of the movie never covered their production costs. In many communities, outraged citizens convinced movie theaters not to show the film; in other cities it closed after boycotts and demonstrations.

All of these tactics are legitimate in a democratic society where people can vote with their pocketbooks. Cries of censorship should not paralyze family-oriented traditionalists from exercising their Constitutional rights to make their views known loud and clear.

For those hesitant to get involved in the public arena, there are other skirmishes that can be fought—in your own home. The TV set is equipped with an off button. Use it. Don't let television become a cheap "babysitter" that quietly imparts a different set of values to your children— values that undercut and undermine everything you try to teach them.

Regulate what movies your children are permitted to see. Be sure you know what they are going to see and be sure other parents know your standards—they cannot take your kids to see shows you do not approve.

Further, follow the movie rating system—as imperfect as it may be. Too many parents are fearful of drawing a line, particularly when peer pressure is pushing your child to see the latest outrage.

It has been said that men and women of character must push as hard as the age pushes against them. Now is the time to push to regain control of your children and the culture.

Gary L. Bauer

13

THE BATTLE
OVER WORDS

All of us remember the old bromide, "Sticks and stones may break my bones, but words will never hurt me." It was a good defense against the hurting taunts of classmates. But words *do* matter, particularly to our children. Words are the currency of discourse. They carry ideas from the speaker or writer to the listener. Words shape the debate.

In our modern political world, politicians are particularly aware of the importance of words. At the White House, key advisors gather around the table before an important Presidential speech and fight for hours over a single word or phrase. What message does it send? Is it too harsh or too strident?

In political campaigns, obscene amounts of money are given to consultants who claim they can put together the right combination of 15 or 20 words that will guarantee the candidate a "sound bite" on the evening news. A poorly turned phrase or the use of a word in an inappropriate way can end a political career or make its speaker appear insensitive or stupid.

By and large, the days are gone when a statesman crafted his own words into speeches or articles. Half of Washington seems to be made up of wordsmiths who ghost write for the other half of Washington. Words are too important to be left to the candidate himself.

The Value of Words

Remember the phrase "kinder and gentler" that President Bush used to describe what America would be like if he were President? Many political pros feel it delivered exactly the right signal to wavering female voters and helped give them a reason to vote for him. Whether the analysis is true or not, the phrase didn't come to the President as he labored deep into the evening on the speech that would define his program. It came from Peggy Noonan, a bright, young speech writer who can turn a phrase with the best of them. She also created the memorable line, "Read my lips: no new taxes."

In America's cultural civil war, words are the bullets used between the two sides, each contending for the hearts and minds of those Americans who have not made their choice of where to stand. Once again, however, the forces hostile to family, faith, and tradition seem to have the inside track. Controlling most of the major instruments of communication, they are able to manipulate words and their meanings over time, in order to advance the modernist agenda.

The adversary culture understands instinctively ". . . that language shapes thoughts, that choice of words can therefore have political and social consequences, that an impoverished vocabulary can impoverish thought."[1]

And that is exactly what has happened in America in recent years. Almost imperceptibly some words have disappeared from our vocabulary. Words like "virtue," for example, or "chastity," are considered hopelessly out of date. Their use in public debate brings forth a round of snickers and nervous laughter.

There is no logical reason for this development. To be chaste or pure has been a noble goal for thousands of years. One only has to open a newspaper or listen to the first five minutes of the evening news to discover the price we pay for the ignoring of virtue among our public servants. Jefferson said only a virtuous people can remain free. Today, in place of virtue we talk about values and, of course, we are constantly reminded that they are relative. Virtue doesn't lend itself to relativism.

Hard Core Denial

While we are remembering old words, dead before their time, how about "evil"? Evidence of it is everywhere but no one dares speak its name. When a "wolf pack" of teenage boys set upon a nighttime jogger in Central Park, raped her, beat her senseless, and left her lying in a pool of her own blood, the airways and newspapers were filled with explanations.

We were told these were disadvantaged youth, as if poverty could ever justify wanton barbarism. "A crowd psychology took over," said another learned mind. "We must understand the root causes," intoned a talk show guest. Yet no one in the cultural elite was willing to call this act what it surely and unmistakably was—evil.

One of Ronald Reagan's most controversial speeches was delivered at a conference in Florida in which he referred to the Soviet Union as an "evil empire." The full wrath of the secular establishment quickly fell down upon his head. Clearly the Soviet Union is an empire; from Lenin to Stalin to Gorbachev, it has waged countless campaigns against its own citizens that can only be described as evil—including the massacre of more than twenty million dissidents in the years leading up to World War II—but the liberal media was shocked at the President's choice of words.

Even as we write, the Soviet Union seems to be fraying at the edges, and the empire may be crumbling, but the historical record of atrocities and evil are undeniable. But for the President to use the word "evil" to describe this history was to raise an issue the cultural elite cannot tolerate.

If some things, or people, or acts, are evil, then it follows that others are good. This then leads to judgments about how we live our lives and how others live theirs. But the whole message of popular culture is the exact opposite. From the teenagers who rape a defenseless woman and then celebrate the act by singing "rap" songs about it in their prison cell, to the legacy of a totalitarian state responsible for immeasurable pain and suffering, who is to say such things are "evil"? The very word is becoming extinct.

Other words have been replaced by non-judgmental substitutes. Somewhere between 1960 and 1980, "promiscuous" gave way to "sexually active." What a phrase to describe the hopping into bed and meaningless coupling that has caused so much pain, heartache, sickness, and even death in our country. But then again, how can a society talk about promiscuity if it is unable to say that it is a good thing to be faithful or to postpone sexual intercourse until marriage?

If you think ten sexual partners a year is okay, on what grounds can you argue with someone else who believes twenty is acceptable? Unfortunately, for some in our society these are modest numbers. Studies of the earliest victims of AIDS showed that many of them had been involved with more than 300 different sexual partners in the twelve months before coming down with the disease.

The word "pornography" is under similar attack. While most average Americans use this word, or the shorthand abbreviation "porn," most opinion leaders prefer the phrase "sexually explicit." Again, the new phrase is value free, it makes no judgment about the material other than the fact that more flesh is being shown.

In any debate on pornography, there is one phrase that will always be brought up. "Well," the liberal will argue, "one man's pornography is another man's art. Who is to judge?" A culture that cannot say what is obscene, and insist on its definition, is a society in deep moral trouble. One can always find a pervert, of course, who sees art in pictures of a woman or child being bound, tortured, and sexually molested, but a healthy society does not allow a sick mind to dictate its judgments about what should be illegal.

Oh yes, and what about that word pervert? Take a good look at it. I predict it too is on its way to the burial ground of words no longer acceptable. Things and conduct considered perversions just a few years ago are now considered mere "preference" or "orientation." None of us, we are told, has the right to describe someone else's conduct as perverted. We are making a value judgment by using such a word—we are saying it is bad, should be punished, deserves condemnation.

The Long Range Implications

When we lose the ability to use words to make such judgments, the slippery slope becomes extremely steep. At a recent conference of *sexologists*, a paper was delivered suggesting that pedophilia, the sexual attraction some men feel toward prepubescent children, may have to be re-defined as an "orientation" rather than the perversion or sexual deviation it is.

I thought of this intellectual obscenity all through the summer of 1989 as a series of young girls in the suburbs of Washington, D.C. were being molested in a crime wave which culminated in the discovery of the lifeless and violated body of one little girl, dumped on a suburban street. Someone's "orientation" had brought incalculable pain and grief to a child, and to the mother and father who loved her.

The abortion debate is also filled with examples of word manipulation. The press seldom refers to the "pro-life" movement. Instead, they are either labeled "anti-abortion" or incredibly "anti-choice." Dan Rather even referred to pro-life advocates as the "anti-women's rights movement!"

The redefinition of words to make it nearly impossible to define normal and abnormal has been going on for some time. Homosexuality has been considered abnormal throughout the ages. But in 1973, under intense pressure from the homosexual lobby, the American Psychiatric Association redefined homosexuality as pathological only for those who sought psychiatric treatment for it. Two years later, the American Psychological Association followed suit.

This brings us to yet another verbal phenomenon—the recreation of new words—new weapons to be used in the civil war. If homosexuality is not considered abnormal, something else called homophobia is. Homophobia is an abnormal fear of and revulsion to homosexuality. The word is routinely leveled at anyone who opposes the gay rights agenda. It is now commonly used in the leading newspapers in the country and by trendy talk show hosts.

It was not listed in any of the leading dictionaries in 1980, but it is easy to predict that it will be in all major reference books within a few years. Clearly, here is a "sickness" the modernists are willing to identify and hurl at their opponents. Never mind that the research studies show that in 1987, fully 81 percent of the American people believe that it is "always wrong," or "almost always wrong," for two adults of the same sex to have sexual relations.

This redefinition of an old word—homosexuality—
and the creation of a new word—homophobia—is not a
minor event or a mere curiosity. Through these semantic
changes, normalcy is put on the defensive. Parents who
want to resist the demands of the homosexual movement
are easily labeled with a condemning word.

Children, in turn, are quickly taught to accept the new
value system. In a number of schools, new classroom material has already been introduced to teach children that
homosexuality is normal and that those who oppose its
political and social agenda are bigots.

The One Way Mirror

Other words in the public debate seem to be "one way"
words. They are only applied to condemn traditionalists, or
certain conservative values, but they are never used in reverse. In examining these words, we are reminded of Alice's
encounter with Humpty Dumpty in *Through the Looking
Glass*. To an astonished Alice, Humpty Dumpty scornfully
says, "When I use a word it means just what I choose it to
mean—neither more nor less."

"Censorship" is a "one way" word. It is routinely
thrown at citizens who oppose pornography, parents concerned about rock music lyrics, citizen groups who question the appropriateness of some classroom materials, or
grass roots organizations who call for boycotts of products
or material that attack their values. The reverse is never
true. The systematic removal of references to our religious
heritage in history books by publishers is never called censorship. Neither is the harassment or closing by universities of college newspapers which have sprung up in recent
years to promote a traditional agenda.

When mainstream bookstores refuse to carry many
books with Judeo-Christian themes but carry all sorts of

tracts on New Age mysticism, no leading figures take to the airwaves to raise the charge of censorship. Search prime-time TV for examples of religion or religious influences in the lives of the characters. It is rare, though religion is a major factor in the lives of Americans.

Writers, directors, producers all have worked together to create these shows with a secular worldview—but this is not considered censorship. Likewise, libraries often remove religious books offering practical advice on family life reflecting biblical concepts. None dare call it censorship!

How about "pluralism"? It too, seems to be a value word that only one side is required to observe. When bizarre lifestyles are thrust on the rest of us and tolerance or even subsidy is demanded, we are directed by the culture to grant it in the name of "pluralism." When traditional Western culture and literature disappear from our major universities and are replaced by a hodge-podge of Third World poetry and philosophy, it is done in deference to the god of "pluralism."

Pluralism is cited as the reason we must show infinite tolerance for all views and viewpoints—except those based on tradition and a Judeo-Christian ethic. When we argue that parents should have more educational choice so that they can send their children to schools that reflect their values, this is never accepted by the cultural elites as something that should be permitted in the name of "pluralism."

"Sensitivity" is a loaded word, but it defends only one set of views or beliefs. We are urged to be sensitive about what we say about the behavior of our fellow citizens. It is insensitive, for example, to suggest that someone who has irresponsibly "slept around" may deserve the sexually transmitted disease they have contracted.

It is certainly considered insensitive to suggest that abortion is the taking of a human life. We are supposed to be sensitive about how we describe the criminals who prey on innocents in our cities—after all they may come from a group that is discriminated against or is socially disadvantaged. Never mind that their victims are too.

In many schools the pledge of allegiance to the flag has been eliminated—the excuse being that it may be insensitive to the child who rejects what the flag stands for. And, of course, a major reason cited by the courts for rejecting a moment of silence to begin the school day is that the village atheist may be offended. We must not be insensitive even to one individual—unless of course the individual is a traditionalist.

No one worried about the lack of sensitivity shown to Christians by the distribution of the movie *The Last Temptation of Christ*. When a child raised in a traditional home is required to take a value-free sex education course, or be one of only a handful of children who bring in a parental note to be excused from class, no concerns are raised about the insensitive treatment of him, even though he is singled out for ridicule by his peers. It's not considered insensitive to women to show them as mere sex objects and playthings at the local pornography shop.

The Incredible Worth of Words

Words? Mere semantics? No, language is how we in a democracy settle our differences and debate the alternatives. Words inspire or shame—they arouse people to action or lull them to sleep. A demagogue using "mere words" can lead a whole nation into the abyss of a destructive World War, a fact we are painfully reminded of as we watch, 50 years later, newsreels of the rantings of the mad Adolf Hitler.

In George Orwell's futuristic novel, *1984*, we are shown a world where a whole new language has been developed, called "newspeak." The purpose of newspeak is not only to provide a medium of expression, but to make all other modes of thought impossible. It was intended that when newspeak had been adopted once and for all, "a heretical thought . . . should be literally unthinkable. . . ."

Increasingly in the civil war over our families and children, there is an effort to make certain thoughts unthinkable, or at the very least, unsayable. Too many who believe in the old values and their worth have been cowered into silence. Who wants to be called a censor? Who enjoys being accused of violating the unwritten rules of pluralism? How can you talk of virtue when the word has descended to a dusty grave?

Perversion and evil abounds but who will call it what it is? The high ground of rhetorical superiority has been occupied by the cultural elites who would sweep away all that millions of Americans embrace. Will we let them continue to hold that ground?

Gary L. Bauer

14
FAITH OF
OUR FATHERS

On January 28, 1986, the Challenger space shuttle lifted off from Cape Canaveral for another planned mission. On board was an all-American crew, including Christa McAuliffe, a public school teacher from New Hampshire.

In hundreds of schools and thousands of classrooms, TV monitors had been set up so that children could watch the live drama of the first teacher going into space. Sitting in my office as Under Secretary of Education, I too was glued to my TV set. Then I watched in horror as the shuttle burst into flames and exploded, killing the seven brave people on board.

In the hours that followed, television commentators compared the horrible event that had been witnessed by millions of people, including countless children, to the wrenching moment when President John F. Kennedy was assassinated. I have never met anyone who was around at that time (anyone who was at least fifteen years old) who does not remember exactly where they were and what they were doing on November 22, 1963.

I remember very well. I was sitting in my junior high school geometry class when a tearful girl brought a note into the room saying that President Kennedy had been shot. I recall that there was sorrow and fear in the room about what this meant for our nation. But the trauma was eased by our wise teacher. Immediately, he calmed us by asking us to bow our heads in a moment of prayer for the President's family and for our country.

This simple act served to remind us that our lives, as always, were in the hands of a merciful God. It was a natural impulse in a stressful time to seek comfort through faith, and it calmed our fear and sorrow.

Children and adults in thousands of communities joined us in praying that fateful day. But by 1986, that right was no longer available to school children. They were not permitted to react to the Challenger explosion the way their parents had responded to tragedy many years before. Any teacher leading students in prayer would have run the risk of discipline by the school district, or worse, a lawsuit by the American Civil Liberties Union.*

In the days that followed the shuttle explosion, news stories told of the extraordinary measures attempted by school officials in their efforts to help students cope with the shock without violating "separation of church and state." One enterprising principal took his student body out into the school yard where they gathered around the flag pole and sang religious hymns. It was illegal, no doubt.

Others tried group discussions, individual counseling, and patriotic assemblies. But in every case the understanding was clear. Teachers and school administrators knew

---

* **Note:** The anti-school prayer decisions of the Supreme Court were made in 1962, but in 1963 they were still ignored in many, if not most, schools.

that they could not pray on school property without violating the law of the land.

In a single generation, the historic practice of asking for God's help in time of trouble had been surgically removed from the experience of children and absolutely prohibited under penalty of law. This is but one example of the vast changes that occurred in the world of the young during this period of revolutionary upheaval. It is time now to pause and look at what else we have lost.

Our History

It is a strange paradox that militant secularism has advanced so far in a nation conceived by the founding fathers to be a haven of religious liberty.

America was built on the idea that we were a nation smiled upon by a loving and protective God. Governor Winthrop, as he crossed the Atlantic on the *Arabella,* wrote in his diary, "We shall be as a city upon a hill, the eyes of all people are upon us."

George Washington at the end of the Revolutionary War stated that our greatest blessing was "the pure and benign light of revelation." He later prayed that God "would most graciously be pleased to dispose us all to do justice, to love mercy, and to demean ourselves with that charity, humility, and pacific temper of mind which were the characteristics of the Divine Author of our blessed religion, and without a humble imitation of whose example we can never hope to be a happy nation." His language was formal but his intent was clear: the success of our nation depended on God and the principles He taught.

When Washington took the oath of office as President on April 30, 1789, in Federal Hall, New York, he added the words, "I swear, so help me God." Every President since then has repeated them. In his famous First Inaugural, Washington made it clear that he saw God's hand in the establishment of America saying, "Every step by which they [the American people] have advanced to the character of an independent nation seems to have been distinguished by some token of providential agency."

During his administration, the first Thanksgiving proclamation was issued. In his farewell address on September 17, 1776, Washington summarized what he thought America needed, what any nation needed, to survive. He told the nation, "of all the dispositions and habits which lead to political prosperity, religion and morality are indispensable supports."

Nor was Washington out of step with the other founders. Ironically, Thomas Jefferson, who is often cited as the originator of a strict separation of church and state, suggested that the Great Seal of the United States should be a depiction of Moses leading his people to the Promised Land. As the primary author of the Declaration of Independence, Jefferson made clear that our rights come from God, not from other men or governments.

Alexis de Tocqueville, a Frenchman who came to America in the early 1800s to determine the "secret" of our successful democracy wrote, "Upon my arrival in the United States, the religious aspect of the country was the first thing that struck my attention." He added, "Religion in America . . . must be regarded as the foremost of political institutions of that country."

President Lincoln, 70 years later, would refer to us as "the almost chosen people." On April 30, 1863, he called for a National Day of Prayer and Fasting. The Proclamation read in part,

> We have been the recipients of the choicest bounties of heaven. . . . But we have forgotten God. We have forgotten the gracious hand which preserved us in peace, and multiplied and enriched and strengthened us; and we have vainly imagined, in the deceitfulness of our hearts, that all these

blessings were produced by some superior wisdom and virtue of our own. . . . It behooves us then to humble ourselves before the offended power to confess our national sins, and to pray for clemency and forgiveness.

When he issued the Emancipation Proclamation in 1862, President Lincoln not only called on world opinion for support, but he asked God's approval by these words:

I invoke the considerate judgment of mankind and the gracious favor of Almighty God.

Reciting the Evidence

Several excellent books have taken a scholarly look at the religious nature of our country's founding and the role of religion in our history.[1] They did not lack for evidence. We could write page after page of other examples of the strong religious foundation of our nation and its institutions.

Millions of Americans today still see the special hand of God in the affairs of our nation from the founding to the present time. Columnist James J. Kilpatrick, in a July 4th column reflecting on the unusual blessings America has enjoyed, wrote:

The men who met at Philadelphia in the summer of 1787 were part of a sunburst of political genius, fairly to be compared with the glory that was Greece and the grandeur that was Rome. Why was our fledgling nation so fortunate? In a single generation a *benign providence* gave us Washington, Adams, Jefferson, Madison, Hamilton, Jay, Pendleton, Marshall, Wythe, Henry, Mason, Morris, the Randolphs and Pinkneys, wise old Franklin—what a roll call! . . . We still sip from their wine.[2]

Yet among America's elite, the self-proclaimed sophisticates and intellectuals, there has been a constant effort to deny the religious roots of our nation, to promote an extreme policy of the separation of church and state, and to demand that citizens inspired and motivated by their religious faith retreat from the "public square."

This conflict between religion and secularism has been fought in nearly every neighborhood and school in America, as well as in the halls of government, and in our highest courts. Its eventual outcome will determine in a profound way who wins and who loses America's second civil war.

The Supreme Court

Confusion on the issue of separation of church and state is perhaps nowhere more pronounced than in the nation's courts. The Supreme Court, the highest judicial authority of the land, has tied itself into tangled knots over the issue. This is the same judicial body that begins its sessions with a Court crier who enters the chambers proclaiming, "God save the United States and the Honorable Court," and which hears oral arguments in a room adorned by the Ten Commandments.

In spite of these obvious reminders of our nation's history, the Court has issued a series of religious liberty and establishment decisions that defy common sense. In recent years, most of these cases have revolved around when and how religious symbols may be permitted on public property. The battle lines become most obvious during the Christian holidays each year.

Have you noticed that there are a number of predictable events that occur each Christmas? The crowds in the stores grow. Decorations appear on our houses. Christmas trees adorn the land. Thoughts turn to family and faith, and to that blessed moment two thousand years ago when God became man. To celebrate this time of year, city fathers have for two centuries displayed nativity scenes, or "creches." But now, in more recent years, the ever vigilant civil libertarian lawyers have rushed into the courts seeking injunctions and citing "separation of church and state" rulings as justification for destroying public expressions of faith in God.

In the summer of 1989, two such cases found their way to the august chambers of the Supreme Court—both from the city of Pittsburgh. One case involved the display of an 18 foot-high Hanukkah menorah on the steps of the Pittsburgh city hall. The other case involved a nativity scene displayed a few blocks away at a Pittsburgh Courthouse.

After months of speculation about how the Court would deal with these issues, the wise judges announced their decision. The menorah was declared Constitutional by a 6 to 3 vote, but the nativity scene was not, by a 5 to 4 tally. The reader should be assured that this was not evidence of favoritism on the Court to one religious tradition over another. If only the explanation were that simple!

As the Justices explained in page after page of legal gobbledygook, the Hanukkah menorah did not violate the Constitution because it was displayed right next to a decorated tree—a secular symbol of Christmas along with snowmen and reindeer. In other words, the religious symbol was not illegal because it was part of an overall display that was cluttered with enough secular symbols so that the average citizen of Pittsburgh wouldn't believe the city was officially endorsing Judaism.

In contrast, the nativity scene down the block had the misfortune of standing alone with no Constitutional "protection" provided by Frosty the Snowman or Old St. Nick. Thus it was declared unconstitutional. This is legalism run amok.

In a toughly worded statement of dissent, Justice Kennedy charged that the court was setting itself up as "a national theology board" that had to decide "what every religious symbol means." Still another quote by Kennedy described the problem even more accurately.

Kennedy charged that the court was displaying an "obsessive, implacable resistance to all but the most carefully scripted and secularized form of Christmas displays." Further, he said, "It appears the only Christmas the state can acknowledge is one in which references to religion have been held to a minimum."

Repeated cases of this nature, and many other bizarre decisions emanating from the court, can only be explained by a growing hostility to religion and religious belief. It is that hostility that leads such lawsuits to be brought in the first place. Few citizens really believe such displays of religious symbols by city governments are oppressive or violate anyone's rights. They are simply examples of a free nation's celebrations of its traditional holidays.

Going to a Higher Power

Other examples of the assault on religious values concern prayers at school graduations, and at the beginning of high school sporting events, or the singing of carols in a public park. Yet all of these cultural events which have occurred without objection for a hundred years are now being attacked by aggressive lawyers. In response, the great minds of the American judiciary have issued mumbo-jumbo prohibitions to legitimize this kind of overt anti-religious activity.

If the courts really want to lighten their work load, they should use a little common sense and follow columnist George Will's advice. Will suggested these kinds of cases could be disposed of by one sentence, "The practice does not do what the Establishment Clause was intended to prevent—impose an official creed, or significantly enhance or hinder a sect—so the practice is constitutional, and the complaining parties should buzz off."[3]

Will's advice is sound, and in fact, is a rough summary of the court's attitude about religious/state disputes for much of our history. From 1776 through the 1950s, no Supreme Court would have seriously considered affirmation of religious belief on public property to be a violation of the Constitution. Perhaps even more significantly, such cases would have never been brought in the first place—so strong was the conviction that America was at its very core a nation built on principles of faith.

The Consensus Breaks Down

Just how far we have traveled away from the thinking of the founding fathers was clearly demonstrated in the reaction to a speech President Reagan delivered at an ecumenical prayer breakfast in Dallas, Texas, on August 23, 1984. There, the President chose to outline his views on the role of religion in our public life. His remarks relied heavily on the beliefs of our founding fathers. Certainly, what he said was in the mainstream of what nearly all American presidents had believed and stated throughout the history of our nation.

After a few introductory remarks, the President went to the heart of the issue by saying plainly what most Americans have believed since our founding in 1776:

> I believe that faith and religion play a critical role in the political life of our nation and always has, and that the church—and by that I mean all churches, all denominations—has had a strong influence on the State, *and this has worked to our benefit as a nation*. Those who created our country—the founding fathers and mothers—understood that there is a divine order which transcends the human order. They saw the State, in fact, as a form of moral order and felt that the bedrock of moral order is religion.

The President then reviewed some of the trends of recent years to take religion out of public life, and leveled a

serious charge at those who campaigned against voluntary
school prayer. He said,

> The frustrating thing is that those who are attacking reli-
> gion claim they are doing it in the name of tolerance, free-
> dom, and open-mindedness. Question: Isn't the real truth
> that they are intolerant of religion? They refuse to tolerate
> its importance in our lives.

The President finished his speech with the clearest
description we have read from a modern political personality on the subject of church and state:

> We establish no religion in this country, nor will we ever.
> We command no worship. We mandate no belief. But we
> poison our society when we remove its theological under-
> pinnings. We court corruption when we leave it bereft of
> belief. All are free to believe or not believe, all are free to
> practice a faith or not, but those who believe must be free
> to speak of and act on their belief, to apply moral teaching
> to public questions.
>
> I submit to you that the tolerant society is open to and
> encouraging of all religions, and this does not weaken us; it
> strengthens us. . . .
>
> Without God, there is no virtue, because there's no
> prompting of the conscience. Without God, we're mired in
> the material, that flat world that tells us only what the
> senses perceive. Without God, there is a coarsening of the
> society and without God, democracy will not and cannot
> long endure.

The entire episode gave a rare glimpse into the fissure
that splits American society. Wagging heads on university
campuses and on the editorial boards of the country's most
influential newspapers were shocked by the President's
assertions. Since it was an election year, his Democratic
opponent immediately challenged the President's remarks
and a debate followed lasting several days. Finally both
candidates turned to other issues.

On election day the President carried every state south of the Mason Dixon line, and all but one west of the Mississippi River. While many issues were important and played a prominent role in the campaign, many political experts believe that the "role of religion" debate was a major factor in signaling to many voters that one candidate, like them, believed that faith was a central part of American life.

In fact, Ronald Reagan benefitted from a massive shift of Evangelicals and Catholics to his candidacy. The other candidate made a serious miscalculation—perhaps because he incorrectly assumed that the editorial boards of major American newspapers, and the liberal advisors who surrounded him, actually represented American mainstream thinking on this issue. He would have been better off to read a little history. It was Daniel Webster, not Ronald Reagan, who said,

> . . . our ancestors established their system of government on morality and religious sentiment. Moral habits, they believed, cannot safely be trusted on any other foundation than religious principle, nor any government be secure which is not supported by moral habits.

In fact as totalitarianism unravels, even dictators are learning of the price that is paid when religious liberty is suppressed. A highly placed government official in the Soviet Union told an American journalist that the Soviet work ethic had been sapped by the Marxist campaign against religion.

> Why? Because without fear of God there was no respect for the concept of authority and laws, or right and wrong. . . . The intellectual dilemma of these people was very basic: What makes man work? What makes life worth living? Just money? Creature comforts? Competition? Keeping score? Power? Pride? . . . Religion provided a necessary structure, if not inspiration, for life.[4]

In 1990, James Dobson met with Dr. Michael Matskovsky, a sociologist and a member of the Academy of Sciences in the Soviet Union. Dr. Matskovsky, a self-professed atheist, said he had come to the United States in search of what he called "ultimate values."

"We don't believe in your God," the Russian said, "but we in the Soviet Union have lost our faith in communism, which was our God. Now we are looking for something to replace it, and we believe the Ten Commandments would be a good place to begin." Then he made a statement Dr. Dobson says he will never forget: "Moral relativism was the beginning of the Soviet tragedy." How unfortunate that America is steadily sliding into moral relativism at the time our Soviet counterparts are trying desperately to escape from its clutches.

A White House Story

In my 19 years in Washington I have often confronted humanistic and relativistic attitudes among journalists, politicians, and bureaucrats. Some are vehemently anti-religious, skeptical of any faith-based claims, and they see the church as an enemy. Many others, however, suffer from a worse affliction. While not hostile to religion, they perceive that to proclaim or defend a meaningful faith makes one likely to be considered a "boob"—an unsophisticate— a hick.

Fortunately Ronald Reagan not only talked about these issues on the campaign trail, but he acted on them too—particularly when he was given the facts. One of the most memorable examples took place in the Monday "issues lunch" scheduled regularly with the President. As we went around the table one day sharing information with him, a dozen issues raced through my mind that I should bring up. All of them were matters that my colleagues would have accepted as legitimate topics of discussion with the President—except for one that I could not get out of my mind.

A few days earlier I had read of an incident that seemed to symbolize the growing restrictions on religious liberty that were slowly taking hold of American public life. Angela Guidry, a straight-A student and valedictorian at Sam Houston High School in Moss Bluff, Louisiana, was preparing to give the graduation speech for the class of 1987.

While rehearsing in the auditorium, a school official listened with interest and then with alarm. Angela planned to end her speech by telling her fellow graduates that a personal faith in God was the most important thing in their lives. Angela was quickly ordered to drop the concluding paragraph. The school principal explained that someone might be offended by her comments. Angela refused, and as a result she was denied the right to give the graduation address: a right that she had worked very hard for four years to win.

I assumed Angela's high school was afflicted with all the problems in other American schools—drug abuse, teenage pregnancy, drop-outs, discipline problems. Here was a girl who had avoided all of these pitfalls. She was, by the press reports I read, the kind of student which America needs by the millions. Yet school officials saw her as a threat to the "order" of the school. I had no idea whether the educators were motivated by fear of the ACLU or of an adverse reaction from parents.

Actually, the motivation didn't matter. The decision made by the principal was symbolic of thousands of other events that, taken together, shrink the area of American life in which expression of faith is permitted.

I had known and admired Ronald Reagan all my adult life. I knew he would also be offended by this injustice. When Chief of Staff Howard Baker asked for my comments,

I resolved to bring up the issue of Angela, even though I had not received advance clearance to do so.

As I relayed the story to the President, I could sense a discomfort in the room. But Reagan himself listened intently. "Mr. President, this is an issue that we should be discussing and bringing to the attention of the American people. It is unfair, it is unjust, and a violation of Angela's freedom of religion. This incident is a mockery in a country built on the notion that every citizen has a right to express his religious views freely."

When I finished there was some whispering around the table. A few muffled laughs were heard. Most of my colleagues avoided eye contact as I looked at them. What was going on here? Suddenly I realized what was happening. They were embarrassed for me. I could almost read their minds by the looks on their faces. I had brought up a very "un-Washingtonian" kind of issue.

Natural Compassion

Who cares about some kid in rural Louisiana? Getting involved in this matter wouldn't get us rave reviews in the *Washington Post*. This wasn't the kind of issue they talk about at Washington's nightly cocktail parties or at the Kennedy Center galas. I had wasted the President's time with this little bit of trivia.

But then I looked at the President, and in a moment I was reminded of why he was President. All his political life he had spoken for the Angela Guidrys of the country. His speeches appealed for a rebirth of religion in our public life.

"I want to help her," he said. "What can we do?"

After a few minutes, we decided a letter of support commending Angela for her courage would mean a lot. In a day or so it was drafted, went through the clearance system and was finally sent.

It read as follows:

Dear Angela,

I read of the events surrounding your proposed commencement address with considerable interest. Like you, I have long believed in the paramount importance of faith in God.

Angela, your actions on behalf of your religious convictions demonstrate not only the strength and passion of those convictions, but your admirable personal courage in facing those who have challenged you. I know that it is often difficult to stand up for one's beliefs when they are being harshly challenged. But as one who has seen many challenges over a long lifetime, I can assure you that personal faith and conviction are strengthened, not weakened, in adversity.

Nancy and I wish you well throughout your life. God bless you.

> Ronald Reagan
> President of the United States

The letter was undoubtedly significant to Angela and her family, but it produced no major changes. The fact that I had used my precious time with the President to bring it up certainly didn't advance my own cause within the White House. Some of my colleagues were probably even more convinced than before that I was in some vague way out of place, lacking in seriousness, or "unsophisticated."

The latter, by the way, is the worst thing that can be said about a government official in a city that is populated by people full of themselves. But at least, a decent girl who loved God received a letter from the President of the United States, praising her courage. That was its own reward.

If I had lost some prestige in the process, it seemed like a fair trade to me. Angela has since married, and has brought a lawsuit against the school district. It is currently pending in the federal courts. Of course, she can never recapture the opportunity to make the valedictory address, but perhaps her principled stand, bolstered by a letter from the President, will help in some way to reverse the growing hostility to the public expression of faith.

Religion in the Classroom

Unfortunately, the Angela Guidry incident is not an isolated case. In thousands of school districts, officials have discriminated against students attempting to exercise their First Amendment rights. Prayer is not only out of the classroom but has been ruled out of order at high school graduation ceremonies and during half-time at sporting events.

One student was expelled from a Georgia high school for merely passing a note in the hallway notifying another student when a religious club would meet. Teachers praying together on their own time in the teachers' lounge have been reprimanded. Unbelievably, Christmas is now being referred to in many schools as the "winter holiday." And so it goes.

Many of the school officials making these decisions have carried bad Supreme Court decisions to a ridiculous extreme. Some are motivated by fear that their school district will be the target of lawsuits from the ACLU and other anti-religion crusaders. But whatever the reason, our children are being taught that religious expression is second class speech that must be silenced.

The hostility has led to the censoring of textbooks and reference materials used in the classroom. What began in the '60s with Constitutional concerns about state-written, mandated, prayers in school has extended to a general hostility to religious references and Judeo-Christian values in any form. This censorship is particularly evident in textbooks widely used in elementary and secondary classrooms.

One study, by Paul C. Vitz, found that in 570 selections from basal readers, there were no examples of serious

Christian or Jewish religious motivation. Vitz found that no character had a primary religious motivation. Further he writes:

> There are scores of articles about animals, archaeology, fossils or about magic, but none on religion, much less about Christianity.[5]

Textbook writers and publishers breathe the haunted air of anti-religious sentiment. Even if their own values are traditional—which surely in some cases they are—they know what kind of textbook wording could cause a state department of education to reject it. Thus, a form of self-censorship takes place that keeps potentially offensive material out. And since the ideas being omitted are those held by traditionalists, not a word of protest comes from the self-appointed keepers of the Constitutional flame.

One of the stories in a Macmillan sixth-grade reader (*Catch the Wind*) is "Zlateh the Goat," written by Nobel Laureate Isaac Bashevis Singer. A young boy, Aaron, is directed to take the family goat to a butcher in a neighboring village to be sold. On the way, he is lost in a terrible blizzard and must search desperately for help. In Singer's original story this line appears: "Aaron began to pray to *God* for himself and for the innocent animal." But what our children read in the Macmillan textbook is, "Aaron began to pray for himself and for the innocent animal."

Later when the boy and goat find safety in a haystack, Singer writes, "Thank *God* that in the hay it was not cold." Again, the forbidden word is never seen by our children. The textbook publisher changed the line to read, "Thank goodness that in the hay it was not cold." One outraged reviewer seeing this censorship was moved to exclaim, "Good grief, they even have to take God out of 'thank God.'"

Of course, nothing in the law or in the Constitution requires this type of tinkering and the Macmillan Publishing Company ought to be ashamed of itself. An isolated incident like this would be merely irritating; but as part of a pattern that robs our children of their religious heritage and treats references to God as if they were expletives unfit for childhood ears, the incident should be cause for outrage.

Musical Disharmony

Things were quite different in America only 40 years ago. One of the most popular music textbooks in 1946 was *New Music Horizons* published by Silver Burdett Co. Intended for 10 and 11 year-olds, the book introduced children to the folk music and cherished songs from over 40 nations, ranging from England and China to Samoa. In addition, there was a fairly heavy emphasis on classical composers, from Bach to Mozart. It sounds like an ideal choice to be used in our schools today—except for one little "problem." The textbook included over 25 hymns.

On page one, for example, along with a picture depicting the signing of the Declaration of Independence, are the words to the "National Hymn."

> God of our fathers, whose almighty hand
> Leads forth in beauty all the starry land
> Of shining worlds in splendor through the skies
> Our grateful song before Thy throne arise.

Other hymns include, "O God, Our Help in Ages Past," "Come Ye Thankful People, Come," and *"Et Incarnatus Est,"* from the Haydn Mass in B-Flat and *"Adir Hu,"* a Hebrew hymn.

We find no historic evidence that the Republic was placed in jeopardy because of the presence of this little music book in our nation's schools. Many children exposed to it probably learned of other cultures while they were participating in formal music instruction. They were also being taught the love of God as the Father of all men. That such books can no longer be used in our schools under the watchful eyes of ACLU attorneys and the courts is a good indication of just how far we have slipped from a nation with a common culture that could be transmitted to our children.

The Naked Public Square

As religion is driven from our public lives, it creates what Richard John Neuhaus has called the "Naked Public Square." But as Neuhaus pointed out, no public square remains "naked." Neither politics, law, nor government, will tolerate a vacuum. Someone's values, based on some philosophy or worldview, will fill the empty space.

That is precisely what is happening in America today. Militant secularism is filling the void with an empty philosophy that cannot restrain the passions of men. Freedom *of* religion has in many important ways come to mean freedom *from* the influence of religion or from even its presence in our public life.

This trend is not accidental. It is one more example of the clash of forces in American society. Freedom of religion, like family and tradition, stand in the way of those who would remake the world and expand the power of government into every aspect of our lives.

The Religious Right

Much has been written in recent years about the "religious right" and its efforts to become involved in politics. Most of the analyses of this issue strike us as strange. Americans motivated by religious values have always been involved in American government and politics. As we have seen, the majority of our greatest leaders have been those who could invoke the traditions of the Judeo-Christian heritage in their speeches to the American people.

Lincoln's great oratory was heavily peppered with biblical allusions, and the Bible was one of only a few books from which he learned the English language. Likewise, Martin Luther King was a minister. His claim to our public conscience was based on the belief that Black men and women have God-given rights equal to the rights of any other race.

Religion has motivated the average citizen as well. We don't put faith in a separate compartment isolated from our family relationships, our work, or our recreation. Most of the pressing issues facing the nation have a clear moral dimension. How do we get drug use under control? What can we do to help the disadvantaged? How can we convince our children to refrain from promiscuity? How can we ensure that our politicians aren't robbing the public treasury?

Americans may not cite Bible verses when they debate these issues, but they certainly base their opinions on their understanding of "right or wrong." And our moral concepts evolve directly from our religious faith.

Nevertheless, the press speaks of the "religious right" as if we were not entitled to express our opinions or attempt to influence the affairs of government. The U.S. Constitution guarantees freedom of speech and religion, yet it appears that those with a certain conservative outlook are supposed to remain silent. There is a great danger here. If the militant secularists carry the day, no one motivated by religion will be permitted to assert themselves without the fear of being ridiculed as the "religious right" or a religious bigot.

Millions of Americans will become politically disenfranchised. All of us have the right to petition the government, elect like-minded politicians, raise money for political

battles, and speak freely and openly about our beliefs and values. But if the militant secularists have their way, Americans with sincere religious faith will have to retreat to their homes or churches, close the doors, and allow only those who are not "contaminated" by religious belief to make key decisions about the future of the country.

Americans motivated by faith have more to worry about than negative editorials in the mass media and bad legislation passed by Congress. Physical violence has already been used in an effort to intimidate people of faith to stay out of the public policy fight.

A Case of Flagrant Villainy

This violence could clearly be seen in the streets outside St. Patrick's Cathedral in New York on December 10, 1989. On that day, Cardinal John O'Connor, the Archbishop of New York, was celebrating Mass with his parishioners. But the Cardinal had accumulated some enemies in recent months. He had spoken out strongly and often against abortion on demand, against homosexuality and other evils. At the same time, he had demonstrated Christian compassion by ministering to the needs of AIDS patients.

But on that cold and windy Sunday in New York, the Cardinal's compassion counted for nothing. Forty-five hundred demonstrators surrounded the Cathedral, demanding that he stop his sermons and public statements against abortion and the homosexual lifestyle. Some members of the mob broke into St. Patrick's, jostling the worshippers, and yelling unprintable obscenities. Others chained themselves to the pews, blocked parishioners trying to take communion, and even threw a "consecrated host" to the floor.

The *New York Times* buried the story of this outrageous attack on religious liberty of all Americans on its "Metro" pages. None of the major television networks ran stories that night on the incident. No mention of it could be

found in the *Washington Post* or other leading media outlets. Yet this was an unprovoked attack by the forces of militant secularism on religious people.

Imagine if the shoe had been on the other foot. What if a mob of Christians had disrupted a homosexual meeting or attacked pro-abortion advocates? That would have made front page news—the subject of outraged editorials and probably even the subject of a Congressional investigation.

Of course, the assault against St. Patrick's was more than an attack on Cardinal O'Connor or on Catholicism. Every pastor, minister, parish priest, or rabbi who upholds biblical teaching is a potential target for such violence. It would be reassuring to think the radicals filled with hate outside St. Patrick's are limited to the confines of New York City. In fact, in every American urban area there are "foot soldiers" for the civil war against family faith and freedom.

To the disrupters, Cardinal O'Connor's dogma is a threat to their own. One poster said, as though it were an all-sufficient indictment, "Cardinal O'Connor won't teach safe sex." "Safe sex" and the values that underlie it are the great counter-dogma of present-day American culture.

Cardinal O'Connor has devoted millions of his archdiocese's dollars to easing the suffering of people with AIDS, but since he advocated traditional morality, he is a heretic against this counter-dogma. Only the law, which still protects religious freedom, prevents the new inquisitors from working their full will on the offender.

That is intolerable. No American can agree to being disenfranchised or willingly go to the "back of the bus." Citizens motivated by the Judeo-Christian value system must continue to be involved in public politics because it is their Constitutional right. It is also their spiritual responsibility.

Faith

In our secular age the battle rages not only over the question of religion in our public life. The very concept of faith is under attack. Cynicism and unbelief mock faith and the sacrifices it brings forth. Yet no nation can long survive if it does not have among its people a deep reservoir of faith in all its forms. This is especially true for democracies where the will of the people prevails.

In a purely secular sense, faith that things will get better (if not now, then later, and if not for you then for your children) is what motivates millions of people to make countless sacrifices. Faith is the force behind the worker who holds down two jobs so that a son or daughter can be the first in the family to go on to college. It is faith in the notion that hard work and right behavior will be rewarded (in the next life, if not always in this one) that causes us to continue to strive and toil.

Religious faith permits a nation to overcome adversity and to deal with the exigencies of life that cause both individuals and countries to suffer. Faith teaches that life is more than a mad rush for wealth, that sacrifice matters, that some of the most important things men do often cannot be completed in one generation.

It is seldom reported that Stalin, when faced by the onslaught of the Nazi invasion, reopened the churches in Russia and brought the imprisoned bishops and clerics back from Siberia in order to restore faith and hope and passionate resolve in the people. Despite his avowed hatred for Christianity, Stalin knew that only faith in God could give the Russian people hope and courage under adversity. Once Hitler was defeated, however, the church bells were silenced again, because faith also can inspire people to rise up against totalitarian governments!

Faith stands at the other end of the continuum from

the highest value of American intellectuals—an open mind. Faith speaks of certainty, but America's leadership class is never certain about anything that matters. Concepts like good and bad, right and wrong, are a puzzle for most of them. All things are forever questioned—the best minds are believed to be those that never "close" on anything.

Intellectual snobs ridicule the simple faith of common people. Having no faith themselves, they attempt to debunk it when they see it in anyone else.

But faith lives on, comes back from a thousand disappointments, mends broken hearts, holds nations together. True faith will not bend before all the professors, politicians and intellectuals that can be massed against it.

On this issue of faith in American life, we are finally and admittedly optimists. Americans remain a very deeply religious people. When compared with the citizens of any other Western nation, the religious commitment which remains—which is actually growing in America—is astonishing.

G. K. Chesterton's observation that "America is a nation with the soul of a church" is still true today, even if opinion leaders and the cultural elite seems embarrassed by the assertion.

Each summer I have been intrigued when the influx of tourists come to Washington, D.C. Literally millions of Americans leave their homes in every state and travel to the nation's capital to show their children this center of the free world. I love to watch them, wide-eyed, with pride on their faces as they visit the great monuments and statues that dot this historical city.

Often you will notice them with their heads tilted far back, pointing to the top of one monument or another. One day my own eyes followed theirs and I saw what attracted their attention. At the top of nearly every historic building in Washington, from the Supreme Court to the Lincoln Memorial, are stirring words, etched in stone, that pay tribute to the religious heritage so deeply believed by our founding fathers.

Engraved on the cap on the top of the Washington Monument are the words: "Praise be to God." As a tourist climbs the winding stairs inside they see such phrases as "Search the Scriptures," and "Holiness to the Lord."

At the Lincoln memorial the President's words are chiseled into granite: ". . . That this nation, under God, shall have a new birth of freedom, and that government of the people, by the people, for the people, shall not perish from the earth." On the south bank of the Tidal Basin sits the magnificent Jefferson Memorial with Jefferson's words, "Can the liberties of a nation be secure when we have removed a conviction that these liberties are the gift of God? Indeed I tremble for my country when I reflect that God is just, that His justice cannot sleep forever."

If the militant secularists are going to win the battle over faith in America, they will ultimately have to sand-blast half the walls of official Washington. But even then what is etched on the hearts of the great majority of the American people will remain and be passed on to the next generation: the simple belief that we are "One Nation, Under God."

In a 1948 speech, then former President Herbert Hoover put it this way:

> America means far more than a continent bounded by two oceans. It is more than pride of military power, glory in war, or in victory. It means more than a vast expanse of farms, of great factories or mines, magnificent cities, or millions of automobiles and radios. It is more, even, than the traditions of the great tide westward from Europe which pioneered the conquest of this country. It is more than our literature, our music, our poetry. Other nations have these things also . . . . [Here there is] that imbedded individualism, that self-reliance, that sense of service, and above all those moral and spiritual foundations . . . . [The

Quakers I grew up with] were but one atom of the mighty tide of many larger religious bodies where these qualities made up the intangibles in the word, American.

What Do We Want?

Since so much of the war over the role of religion in American life has been fought with inaccurate stereotypes and personal attacks instead of reasoned debate, we want to make clear the position we favor as well as what we oppose.

First, we see the Declaration of Independence as the core document of the American founding. When it says that we are "endowed by the Creator with unalienable rights," it expresses the basis of our liberty. The American experience is built on a key belief—that our rights come from no man, no government, but from God. A rejection of this critical concept by the leadership classes of our nation ultimately puts our liberty at risk.

Second, the founders thought, and we still believe, that our system of government can only function over time if the people it governs are moral and virtuous. A democracy cannot survive if there is nothing to restrain the appetites of its citizens. For us, morality which is based on spiritual beliefs is necessary for the survival of our Republic.

Third, we believe that all Americans are guaranteed the free exercise of religion. Our children do not give up that freedom when they enter the schoolroom door. Nor should any of us be intimidated into silence or refrain from public debate because we are motivated by faith. We reject the notion that religious belief must be always private or that it has no place in the debate over the great issues facing our nation.

We believe the concept of the separation of church and state was intended to prevent government from establishing an official religion; it has been twisted into outright hostility to religious beliefs.

Fourth, we believe that our children must be taught an accurate history of religion's role in the beginning of our nation as well as in the great social and political reform movements of our 200-year history, from the abolition of slavery to the Civil Rights movement.

We do not believe that one particular religious faith should be promoted in the public schools—but we do believe children of all faiths in those schools have a right to pray singly or together and have the same rights of free speech and free access to school property as do students promoting secular thoughts and arguments.

We do not believe that only Christians should hold public office but we do believe that the moral and ethical conduct of those who aspire for high elective office are legitimate issues to be discussed in the political process. We believe our nation is founded on the Judeo-Christian ethic, but we welcome other citizens who come from a different religious tradition and are attracted to America as a haven where they can practice their own faith without fear of persecution.

We believe that the overwhelming majority of Americans agree with these principles. Yet in every case, the views we have embraced are on the defensive from a concerted attack by forces hostile to religious belief. We do not intend to see that situation long continue.

James C. Dobson

15

WHERE DO WE GO FROM HERE?

For those readers who have journeyed with us through this alarming and sometimes distressing battle report, we want to express our appreciation and regards. We have dealt with a topic many Americans in the past have preferred to avoid, but that reluctance to face reality seems to be changing. And for good reason.

Today, everyone can see we're in a mess. The question is, how will we get out of it? Where will we turn for answers to the problems created by the social engineers?

Certainly those who gave us such great ideas as the sexual revolution and rampant individualism now stand ready to offer new solutions. In fact, they see the crisis in today's families as an opportunity to promote even crazier ideas. Suggestions that would have brought instant ridicule a few years ago are now given respectability in this no-holds-barred kind of world.

Perhaps you will remember, for example, an article published in the April 2, 1990, issue of *Newsweek* magazine. The author, Noel Perrin, offered a new approach to solving America's "overpopulation problem." Perrin suggested that the federal government pay every prepubescent girl $400 for not getting pregnant for one year—or should we say, for not *staying* pregnant.

The writer suggested that in the second year the girl should receive $500, then $600 the third, and so on until she is 52 years of age. If she chooses to remain barren for life, she would receive nearly $100,000 for her non-productivity. No fooling! That is what this man wrote, apparently without flinching, and at a time when the birth rate in America has already dropped below the zero population growth level. Based on birth rate, the population of this country is actually in decline.

It is not so amazing that one confused freelance writer could dream up such a stupid idea. What astounds me is that a magazine like *Newsweek* would publish it, and that its readers would take the author seriously. Indeed, some crazed California assemblyman promptly drafted the concept into a bill that was mercifully voted down by the state legislature.

Consider the world Perrin would have imposed upon us—a society with few or no children to raise. If the system of rewards succeeded even for a few years, there would soon be no maternity wards, no pediatricians, no toys, no tricycles, no schools, no children's literature, no little ones around our feet to love and train and protect.

All that would remain in a decade or two would be a society of utterly selfish adults, steadily moving toward death with no hope of youthful regeneration. The Creator's most precious gift of procreation would be but a memory. And how could the nation hope to protect itself militarily or even provide the bare necessities for its aging citizens as the pruning knife of time cut them down? Noel Perrin has offered us a prescription for social suicide—all for a mere $114 billion. What a bargain!

But Perrin is not the only bright-eyed humanist to come up with off-the-wall solutions to the mythological "overpopulation problem." Remember Gary's shocking experience at the White House with the politician who wanted to put infertility drugs in the water? Although Gary chose not to identify this man, he was one of the up-and-coming young members of the Republican Party. God help us!

This is where secular humanism leads when given free reign. This is the convoluted thinking that exudes from the grave of dead faith. When men depart from the time-honored wisdom of the Scriptures and disregard the God of the universe, they cease to make sense.

Dying from Within

The late philosopher, Francis Schaeffer, was one of the first to recognize that secular humanism is a cultural disaster in the making. No matter how intelligent it appears at the time, it is hopelessly inadequate as a system of values.

Schaeffer offered this very perceptive illustration. He said there are bridges scattered across Europe that were built by the Romans during the flourishing of their Empire. Amazingly, these unreinforced structures are still standing today, nearly 2,000 years later. The reason for their longevity is the careful way they are used. Only *people* are permitted to cross them. If they were used by trucks or heavy equipment, they would come down in a sudden avalanche of brick and mortar.

Secular humanism, said Schaeffer, is like those antique bridges. It *appears* to be secure and stable during good times. However, if unusual pressure is placed on this unreinforced system of values, the entire superstructure can come crashing down. A war, an economic crisis, or some other social unrest will eventually destroy a democracy based on the shifting sands of human wisdom. That is what we are seeing year by year in the steady decline of Western civilization.

As Gary and I have attempted to illustrate in each of these chapters, it is our children who are the most tragic victims of this disintegration. The young are always the first to suffer in a full-scale civil war. But who could have imagined just a few years ago how terrible would be their pain!

Who would ever have imagined that the numbers of babies and youngsters who are afflicted by crack-cocaine, maternal alcoholism, sexually transmitted diseases, child molestation, physical abuse, abandonment, and neglect would be so enormous? The sorrow we inflict on our children is a national disgrace. For those who escape these tragedies of early childhood, there is the spiritual and ethical confusion inevitable in a relativistic world.

Consider the results of a survey conducted in 1988 by the Rhode Island Rape Crisis Center. Some 1,700 students between the sixth and ninth grade attended adolescent assault awareness classes conducted in schools across the state. Each boy and girl was asked if a man should have a right to *force* a woman to have sexual intercourse if he had spent money on her.

The results were shocking. Nearly 25 percent of the boys and 16 percent of the girls said "yes"! Then 65 percent of the boys and 47 percent of the girls in seventh through ninth grades said it is okay for a man to force a woman to have sex with him if they have dated for six months or longer. And 51 percent of the boys and 41 percent of the girls said a man has a right to force a woman to kiss him if he spent "a lot of money on her"—which was defined by 12-year-olds as $10 to $15.[1]

I must admit to being shocked by these findings, and yet, not really. These young students merely learned the lessons they were taught by the value-free educational system.

Their teachers taught them in sex education classes that there is *nothing* right or wrong, no standard for moral judgment. "It all depends on how *you* see the matter, Johnny." It turns out Johnny sees it rather brutally.

Johnny's older brothers learned their lessons well, too. In a classic study at UCLA, Malamuth and Feshbach found that 51 percent of male sophomores said they would rape a woman if they knew they would never get caught.[2] This is the legacy of moral relativism, just one generation removed.

Designer Abortions

Death is also its natural consequence. Perhaps the most startling information now coming to light is news of so-called "designer abortion" occurring around the country. Amniocenteses are performed to determine the sex of the child, then the mother may elect to abort the child if she is not satisfied with what she got. Far more often than not, the babies being killed are female. This is a moral outrage and the ultimate assault on "women's rights."

Femicide, as it has been termed, will almost certainly result in significantly fewer females in the world of the future. In Korea, for example, the sex ratio resulting from designer abortions went to 117 males for every 100 females before the testing of fetal sex was declared illegal. In China, where female babies are often drowned, a disastrous imbalance is apparently in the making. Results from China's 1987 census indicate that single men between the ages of 25 and 39 outnumbered single women by a ratio of 689 to 100.[3]

The siege of unbridled individualism has also left its trail of death and destruction on the landscape. I'm reminded of Gaetan Dugas, a Canadian airline steward who best represents the promiscuous and anti-traditional spirit of the past thirty years. Among public health officials studying the early spread of the HIV virus, Dugas earned the name "Patient Zero."[4]

Time after time, those dying of AIDS in cities from New York to San Francisco included his name in their list of sexual partners. Public Health officials speculate that he was probably one of the first to bring the virus into North America, and certainly played a major role in its spread through the homosexual communities of several cities.

Incredibly, even when Dugas realized he was spreading a deadly disease, he continued to frequent homosexual bath houses and to engage in high-risk activity. When a San Francisco public health official told him in 1982 to stop this dangerous behavior, Patient Zero is alleged to have reacted with anger and shouted, "It's my right to do what I want to do with my own body."

It would be difficult to recite a more accurate banner to hang over the social and political landscapes of recent years. "My right," "my body," "do what I want"—this is the new trinity of the modern age. From abortionists to pornographers; from homosexuals to drug users; all have claimed the right to do what they want with their own bodies. No one was supposed to "judge" anyone else.

But we are slowly learning that "private" acts have public consequences. Patient Zero's right to promiscuous sex transmitted death to his partners and eventually to children like the courageous teenager, Ryan White. No one knows what the final death toll from the AIDS disaster will be, but some experts believe it will be the worst epidemic in human history.

Regaining America's Historic Values

The examples of humanistic folly have been legion in recent years. The only logical answer is to return America to the Judeo-Christian values system with which we started! It served us so well, from the landing of the Pilgrims at Plymouth Rock through the "Happy Days" of the 1950s. This worldview bears the unique stamp of the

Creator, Himself, who injected a bit of His own infinite wisdom into its veins. Our best hope is to reinstate its precepts into government, the schools, and into our homes.

We are not naive in this expectation, however. A sudden shift of public opinion in the direction of yesteryear would probably only occur in the event of a natural catastrophe. Or, to apply our bellicose analogy, civil wars rarely end with capitulation of the side that is winning.

What is necessary in the absence of that quiet revolution, is for those who agree with what we have written to enlist in the struggle. Such common sense people represent the vast majority of Americans and they scare the daylights out of the liberal elite. If they are ever aroused, the tide of battle could change in a matter of days!

To our way of thinking, *women* are the key to this contest. Whether at home or in the work force, many of them have seen firsthand the effects of our flight from family and faith. What an incredible army these millions of mothers could be, most of whom believe in responsible living, in traditional standards of right and wrong, and in the God of our fathers.

Countless numbers of men out there feel the same way, although fewer have stopped to consider the matter as closely. To all of you moderately conservative people who have been thinking about something else, we implore you to get involved. Six hundred thousand men had to die before the curse of slavery was eliminated from this great land. It will take far more men and women today who are willing—not to lay down their lives—but to *invest* them in our future and in the well-being of our children.

If you do nothing, your grandchildren are likely to grow up in the world crafted by the social engineers. Who knows what the family will look like when they've had their way? Who can imagine what children will be taught in public schools of that brave new world? Who could guess how many will die when the death-with-dignity crowd has written our laws? Who will we blame when every child is placed in mandatory state-run nursery schools? These and a hundred other nightmares can still be prevented, but there is no time to lose.

To those who want to use their influence, we must outline the changes needed most urgently. There are, it would appear, five key objectives that could make the greatest difference. We've already described the first, which is (1) to get personally involved in the battle to save the family. Let's discuss now the second and third goals, which are (2) clean house in Washington, D.C., and (3) lower the tax rate on families.

Playing the Odds

The nation's capital is so thoroughly anti-family and *ignorant* of the family that traditional lobbying techniques will not be sufficient. Lobbying is important in the short term, of course, as are letters and calls to our representatives. But a better plan of attack is needed. Let's look at the odds.

It is estimated that 20 percent of our congressmen and senators are solidly pro-family most of the time. They can be counted on to defend traditional values even when it is not popular to do so. Perhaps 40 percent, at the other end of the spectrum, are committed to the liberal agenda. They can be counted on to support anti-family legislation at every turn. No amount of influence or lobbying effort will divert them from this philosophical objective.

That leaves 40 percent in the wishy-washy middle. These congressmen and senators have no definite commitment to anything except getting reelected. They vote this way or that, depending on how they read the political thermostat.

Forty-four of these fair-weather friends revealed their opportunistic nature in 1989. They had voted pro-life consistently in the past, some of them for years. But then the media launched a massive propaganda campaign after the Supreme Court's *Webster* decision, and they ran for cover, like scared rabbits. The next time an abortion issue came up for a vote, these 44 "statesmen" switched to the "pro-choice" side. Doesn't that say it all?

If the killing of babies is wrong and immoral, as they agreed prior to 1989, how could it suddenly be right and holy? It would appear that these middle-ground politicians would rather get re-elected than to stand for anything— except another election.

What we are suggesting is that at least ten to twenty percent of these members of Congress, and perhaps six senators, should be sent into early retirement. That's all it would take to awaken the rest. Nothing will reinstate pro-family values in the Congress except this kind of conservative victory on election day. Until that happens, our representatives will "hear" only those special interest groups who *are* willing to work for or against their job security.

We must also be willing to work for and against our state representatives. Governmental analysts tell us more and more decisions will be made in the future at the local level, as the federal system bogs down in bureaucracy. Certainly, the abortion issue will be decided by each state in this post-Webster era. That's why we must not focus our attention only on Congress and its impact on families.

Your support of pro-family state representatives will be warmly appreciated by local elected officials, I'm sure. They are desperately in need of encouragement. A California assemblyman told us recently of the special frustrations he faces in his efforts to defend traditional values. He said when he votes in opposition to one of the militant groups, such as gay-rights activists, the gays will send 500 troops into his district who will go door to door talking about him.

They wouldn't dare say, "Hi, I'm Jack, I'm gay and I'm unhappy with Assemblyman Rogers because he is not treating us right." Instead, they tell people their representative is against the elderly, is wasting state money, and has defunded valuable programs for handicapped kids.

This assemblyman told us it takes him months to recover from an assault of that nature in his district. On the other hand, when he votes for important pro-family legislation, he may receive a handful of appreciative letters. That's the end of it. This, along with the power of the liberal press, explains why so many politicians gravitate inexorably to the other side.

Containing the Costs

A third objective for our side at both the national and state levels is to achieve a lower tax rate on individual families. Lower taxes will mean preserving more of the family's income, and that, in turn, will permit husbands and wives to decide for themselves on the issue of outside employment for mothers. Let us be clear at this point. It is the choice of many women to have ambitious careers, and we wish to make no comment on their decision to do so. It is not our purpose or privilege to say what family members should do with their lives.

On the other hand, the surveys and polls consistently show that there are millions of employed women who want nothing more than to be at home with their children. The mail that we receive at Focus on the Family verifies this frustrated desire by so many mothers in the work force. Given that easily verifiable fact, how dare congressmen and state representatives deny women that option by the excessive taxes they impose on families! What arrogance to give tax breaks to special interest groups and ignore the largest constituency in the land!

To those who speak of federal deficits and the inability of government to meet all the demands made upon it, just remember this: Congress wastes untold billions of dollars on nonsense that would make us ill if we fully understood. Take a look at the congressional retirement program, for example. Many public servants will receive more than a million dollars after they leave office. One retired senator receives $136,000 per year—$37,000 more than he would earn if he were still on the payroll. This symbolizes government's inclination to feather its own nest at the expense of the average taxpayer.

To give a $7,000 deduction for each dependent would cost an estimated $40 billion per year, but it would permit millions of mothers to stay at home if they choose to do so. A lot of money? Yes. But Congress allocated $27 billion for child care without flinching in 1989, and tens of billions more for public works, water projects, and old-fashioned "pork barrel." Money is sprayed like water from a firehose on everything but the institution of the family. Mom and dad are expected to keep their mouths shut and to go on paying the bill. But we're here to say, "Enough is enough!"

Let's turn our attention now, briefly, to the next suggestion that we consider critical to the preservation of our children: (4) reorganize the funding for public education.

We believe a voucher system is the key to improving our nation's educational system. It would permit parents to choose the particular schools they want their children to attend, whether public or private. This is a controversial proposal that is opposed by many of our friends in the field of education. I'm not sure I blame them. Schools now have a monopoly that assures them students and income. It is also a system that guarantees mediocrity.

What has made American business the most efficient in the world has been the constant stimulus of healthy competition. That is the heartbeat of the American system of democratic capitalism. Companies that succeed are those which serve the consumer and deliver the goods. If you want a good look at how poorly monopolies work, just try to renew a drivers license at the California Department of Motor Vehicles. It is an administrative nightmare. Long lines, sometimes rude clerks, and lost records are the rule. But who cares? There is no competition that will take customers away. They have millions of them!

Educational Free Enterprise

The beauty of the free enterprise system is that it pits the wisdom, ingenuity, hard work, and dedication of one entrepreneur against his competitor across town. Yes, the loser may be driven out of business, but the big winner is the consumer. It is time for the educational consumer—the parent—to be served by an enthusiastic, entrepreneurial school district that desperately wants to please him or her.

In short, the advantage of a voucher system is that it places a small amount of power in the hands of parents. Heaven knows, they need it today. We continue to hear from mothers and fathers who are unable to get the attention of their children's educators. "Just leave the schooling of your children to us," they are told. At least that is the attitude parents sense.

But a mother or father with a voucher in hand is suddenly transformed into a customer with "money" to spend. The entire relationship is changed. We believe schools will be better for it. If, for example, an offensive sex education program could be expected to cause 300 parents to choose another school alternative, you can be sure moderation would prevail.

Admittedly the implementation of a voucher system is not a cure-all. Schools are a reflection of the societies in

which they function. Thus, many of the difficulties occurring in public education are *our* problems, collectively.

It would be unfair to blame the many dedicated and
hard-working teachers for the wounded children who
show up in their classes each day. Only when we address
the broader issues of drug abuse, alcoholism, shattered
families, and others, will test scores and general education efficiency return to our nation's schools. Even if those
problems are not solved, however, the application of a
voucher system is a great step in the right direction.

Linking Up, and Looking Up

In the meantime, we strongly advise parents to link
arms with other families in dealing with school administrators. A one-on-one interchange in response to serious
disagreement can be frustrating. All the power is on the
side of the school. *Organization* is the only way to balance
the scales.

Finally, I want to recommend an incredibly valuable
program for women called "Moms-in-Touch." More than
50,000 mothers assemble each week through the ministry
of Moms-in-Touch for the purpose of praying for their children, their teachers, the local school principal, the superintendent, the board of education, and others.

These women are not politically motivated. They fuss
with no one. They use no pressure techniques. They simply
gather together to pray for the local school. And *remarkable*
things happen when they do. For information, write to:

Moms-in-Touch
P. O. Box 1120
Poway, California 92074

You may also request a taped interview on the subject
from Focus on the Family, Pomona, California 91799.

The fifth proposal is a simple idea but one that must not be overlooked. Our children need formal, well-designed instructional programs regarding the issues that affect them. By the time they are in junior high school, they should know what the family believes, and why they believe it. They should be taught the dangers of pornography, the evils of abortion, the risk of AIDS and venereal disease, the importance of premarital virginity, the damage done by heavy metal music, the debate over creation vs. evolution, and the objectives of the gay-rights movement.

They should also hear the basic differences between the Judeo-Christian and humanistic worldviews. Those who would capture the hearts and minds of your kids certainly have a plan to get across what they want them to know. What countermeasures have you taken? Can we afford to prepare more haphazardly than they? Certainly not!

One of the best programs for teaching the concepts I've described is called the Summit Ministries, located in Manitou Springs, Colorado. Run by Dr. David Noebel, it is designed to prepare 15 to 25 year-old students to deal with the secular humanism they will certainly encounter in high school or college. It is an economical, two-week program each summer that "pops open" the eyes of teenagers and young adults.

They suddenly understand the civil war we have described and what it means to them personally. Furthermore, although most kids have to be required to attend, 96 percent say they love being there. Our son, Ryan, has attended the past three summers. He recommends it, too. For information, write to:

Dr. David Noebel
Summit Ministries
Box 207
Manitou Springs, Colorado 80829.

While we're listing important resources, let me emphasize the importance of accurate and up-to-date information about the battle to save the family. The second great civil war will not be won by a sleepy-eyed army of poorly informed and woefully disorganized spectators. We must understand the issues. We must know where reinforcements are needed. We must be able to coordinate our efforts. We must have facts! Unfortunately, little help of that nature has been available until recently.

That situation led Focus on the Family to begin producing both a magazine and a radio program designed to keep us informed. *Citizen* magazine is a monthly publication with a circulation of 300,000 that is available for a contribution of $15 per year. I'm biased, of course, but I believe it is the best source of information of its type anywhere. The radio broadcast, "Family News in Focus," offers the same kind of insightful news and commentary on some 500 stations. To learn about either of these resources, contact:

Focus on the Family
Pomona, California 91799.

How about information relevant to what's happening in Washington? There is help here, too. Focus on the Family is a non-profit organization that takes no position on office holders or candidates for political office. We *can,* however, provide objective information detailing how congressmen and senators are doing on family-related issues. The *Washington Watch* newsletter does that and is available for $7.00, from:

Family Research Council
700 13th Street NW, Suite 500
Washington, D.C. 20005.

Finally, we come to the closing words of this book and the most important recommendation we have to offer. Our only hope as a nation, ultimately, is to ask the Father to forgive our sins and heal our great land. He blessed this country from its infancy with some of the most gifted leaders every produced by any fledgling nation.

As we have seen, virtually all of the founding fathers revered the Lord and looked to Him for strength and wisdom. They inscribed "In God We Trust" on our coins. It was they who said, "We are endowed by the Creator with certain unalienable rights." It is clear from the record they left that our early leaders knew in Whom they believed, and no amount of modern-day revisionism can change that historical fact.

Today we cling to the same source of confidence and hope. Yes, our families are pitching and rolling like ships on a stormy sea. But we believe they can be sailed again into the safe harbor of peace and harmony.

We must appeal again to Him who promised in the concluding words of the Old Testament, "He will turn the hearts of the fathers to the children and the hearts of the children to their fathers" (Malachi 4:6 KJV). That would be great news, indeed, for the families of the world.

NOTES

Chapter 1
 1. James Dobson, *Parenting Isn't for Cowards* (Word, Inc., 1987) pp. 13, 14.

Chapter 2
 1. The California legislature subsequently adopted the Civil Code Section 43.6 in 1981 to prevent handicapped children from suing their parents for permitting birth to occur, although similar "wrongful life" rulings have been handed down in other courts.
 2. Reuters News Service, February 21, 1990.
 3. Incidentally, you may know that the Supreme Court ruled in *Miller vs. California, 1973*, that obscenity is not protected by the First Amendment and that the definition of obscenity is determined by "community standards." When leftist lawyers defend pornographers against these laws, they usually argue that there *are* no community standards . . . no concensus on what is patently offensive.
 4. *San Francisco Chronicle*, July 18, 1990.

Chapter 3
 1. James Hitchcock, "Competing Ethical Systems," *Imprimis*, April 1981, Copyright 1981, Hillsdale College.
 2. Mary S. Calderone and Eric W. Johnson. *The Family Book About Sexuality* (New York: Harper and Row, 1981) p. 171.
 3. Jacqueline Kasun, "Sex Education: A New Philosophy for America," *The Family in America*, July 17, 1981, p. 1.
 4. Pomeroy, Wardell B., *Boys and Sex*, Delacorte Press, a Division of Bantam Books.
 5. Pomeroy, Wardell B., *Girls and Sex*, Delacorte Press, a Division of Bantam Books.
 6. "Date Rape," *Ms.* magazine, October 1985, p. 84.
 7. *The Proposition*, January, 1990, The Claremont Institute, "A Terrible Disappointment." Dr. Jaffa is an emeritus professor of political philosophy at Claremont McKenna College, and Director of the Claremont Institute's Center for the Study of Natural Law.

Chapter 5
1. "Government Must Strengthen Family," *U.S.A. Today,* Nov. 21, 1986, p. 12A.
2. "Back to the Future Family," *The Detroit News,* Dec. 8, 1986.

Chapter 6
1. "Looking to Harriet," Daniel Seligman, *Fortune Magazine,* July 17, 1989, p. 117.
2. Diane Katz, "Who is Minding The Kids? Working Parents Worry," *The Detroit News,* May 22, 1988.
3. Paper by David Blankenhorn, "American Family Values," delivered at Stanford University, November 1989, p. 9.
4. Paper by David Blankenhorn, "American Family Values," delivered at Stanford University, November 1989, p. 9.
5. Spencer Rich, "Hyping the Family's Decline," *The Washington Post,* July 26, 1987.
6. *Miguel Braschi vs. Stahl Associates Company,* State of New York Court of Appeals, No. 108, p. 9.
7. *Moore vs. City of East Cleveland,* 431 U.S. 501, 506 (1977).
8. Editorial: "Devaluating Matrimony," *New York Post, June 12, 1989.*

Chapter 7
1. Mary McGrory, "The Child Care Battle Is Over," *The Washington Post,* June 30, 1988.
2. Don Feder, "Child Care Threatens Ecology," *The Boston Herald,* Nov. 2, 1989, p. 47.
3. Christopher Lasch, *Haven in a Heartless World* (New York; Basic Books 1977), p. 137.
4. Alan Wolfe, "The Day-Care Dilemma: A Scandinavian Perspective," *The Public Interest,* No. 95 (Spring 1989), p. 17.
5. P. Barglow, B.E. Vaughn and N. Molitor, "Effects of Maternal Absence Due to Employment on the Quality of the Infant-Mother Attachment in a Low Risk Sample," *Child Development,* 58 (1987) pp. 945–954.
6. William R. Mattox, Jr., "Day Care Diseases, Exploring the Risks of Center Based Care," *Family Policy,* May/June 1989.
7. Nancy Hathaway, "Working Mothers Does Your Child Need Now?" *Harper's Bazaar,* July 1988, p. 143.
8. "I Am a Woman," ©1961, 1963 (Renewed) Jerry Leiber Music & Mike Stoller Music.

9. Andrea Boroff Eagan, "Long vs. Short Maternity Leaves," *Glamour*, March 1986, p. 214 ff. Cited in Maggie Gallagher, *Enemies of Eros* (Chicago; Basic Books, 1989), p. 93.

10. "How Women View Work. Motherhood and Feminism," *Newsweek*, March 31, 1986, p. 51.

11. "Child Care: A Problem or a Voting Issue?," *Public Opinion*, (July/August 1988), p. 36.

12. Karl Zinsmeister, "Brave New World: ;How Day Care Harms Children," *Policy Review*, (Spring 1988), p. 45.

13. Brenda Hunter, "Attachment and Infant Daycare," pp. 65–67, in *Who Will Rock the Cradle?* (Dallas: Word, 1989).

Chapter 8

1. Whittaker Chambers, *Witness* (South Bend, Indiana; Regnery/Gateway 1979), pp. 325–326.

2. Dr. Leo Alexander, "Medical Science Under Dictatorship," *New England Journal of Medicine*, 241 (July 14, 1989) pp. 39–47.

3. Nat Hentoff, "Small Beginnings of Death," *Human Life Review*, Vol. 14, No. (Spring 1988), p. 54.

4. Victor Cohen, "Is It Time for Mercy Killing?" *The Washington Post*, August 15, 1989.

5. Daniel Callahan, *Setting Limits* (New York; Simon & Schuster, 1987).

6. William A. Donohue, *The New Freedom* (New Brunswick, New Jersey: Transaction, 1990), p. 62.

7. Cohen.

8. Ronald Reagan & Malcolm Muggeridge, *Abortion and the Conscience of the Nation* (New York; Thomas Nelson, 1984) pp.82–83.

9. Kathleeen Kerr, "Baby Doe's Success," *Newsday*, Dec. 7, 1987, p. 1.

Chapter 9

1. Dinesh D'Souza, "The New Feminist Revolt," *Policy Review*, No. 35 (Winter 1986), p. 47

2. Betty Friedan, *The Feminine Mystique* (New York: Norton, 1963), pp. 217–336

3. Suzanne Fields, "When Instincts and Stereotypes Embrace," *The Washington Times*, April 17, 1990, p. F1

4. "Got That Right," *The Washington Times*," Sept. 21, 1988.

5. Paul C. Vitz, *Censorship: Evidence of Bias in our Children's Textbooks* (Ann Arbor: Servant Books, 1986).

6. Maggie Gallagher, *Enemies of Eros* (Chicago: Bonus Books, 1989), p. 9.

7. Yevgeny Zamyztin, *We* (New York: Avon Books, 1987), p. 216.

8. Ladies Home Journal, March 1989, p. 70.

9. Dr. Joyce Brothers, "Why Wives Have Affairs," *Parade* magazine, February 18, 1990, pp. 4–7.

10. David Blankenhorn, "What Do Families Do?," paper presented at Stanford University, November 1989, p. 19.

11. William J. Bennett, *Our Children and Our Country* (New York: Simon & Schuster, 1988), p. 64.

12. Nicholas Davidson, "Life Without Father," *Policy Review*, No. 51 (Winter 1990), p. 42.

13. Toni Morrison, interview in *Time* magazine, May 22, 1989, p. 122.

Chapter 10

1. David Hoffman, "President Calls on Schools to Teach the 'Basic Values,' *The Washington Post*, August 24, 1984, p. A7.

2. For a full account of the test results and their implications, see *What Do Our 17-year-olds Know?* by Diane Ravitch and Chester E. Finn, Jr., (New York: Harper & Row, 1987).

3. John Leo, "Teaching History the Way it Happened," *U.S. News & World Report*, Nov. 27, 1989.

4. Gerald Sirkin, "The Multiculturalists Strike Again," *The Wall Street Journal*, January 18, 1990.

5. Amy Goldstein, "College Seniors Fall Short on Humanities Questions," *The Washington Post*, Oct. 9, 1989. p. A4.

6. *Washington Times*, April 2, 1990, p. A8.

7. George Will, "Education of the Moment," *The Washington Post*, May 6, 1984.

8. Tamara Jones, "Wounded Marine Scrawls 'Semper Fi' to His Boss," *The Washington Post*, October 26, 1983.

9. Will and Ariel Durant, *The Lessons of History* (Simon & Schuster 1968), p. 102.

Chapter 11

1. Henry J. Hyde, "The Culture War," *National Review*, April 30, 1990, p. 25.

2. Maureen Dowd, "Jesse Helms Takes No-Lose Position on Art," *New York Times*, July 28, 1989, p. A-1.

3. Suzanne Muchnic, "Conference on the Arts Tackles First Amendment Issues," *The Los Angeles Times*, Feb. 17, 1990, p. F6.

4. Michael Mehle, "Federal Funding for Arts Backed," *Knight-Ridder News Service*, March 30, 1990.

5. Frederick E. Hart, "Contemporary Art Is Perverted Art," *The Washington Post*, August 22, 1989.

6. Walter Laqueur "Weimer: A Cultural History 1918–1933." (A Perigree Book, 1973) Quoted by John Lofton in the *Washington Times* 7/7/89 "A Time When Beauty Was a Lie."

Chapter 12

1. Testimony before the Senate Subcommittee on Family and Human Services, March 22, 1983.

2. T.V.: Limit Kids to Two Hours. *USA Today*, 4/17/90, p. A1.

3. Parents Poll, "Should Parents Be Censored?" by Ingrid Groller, April 1990, p. 34.

4. Quoted in The Family: Preserving America's Future, Report to President Ronald Reagan, p. 29.

5. "Leaving Religion Out of the Picture" by Donna Britt, *USA Today*, 8/30/88.

6. Linda S. Lichter, S. Robert Lichter, and Stanley Rothman, "Hollywood and America: The Odd Couple," Public Opinion, December/January 1983, p. 56.

7. "More Kafka than Capra" by David Brooks, *National Review*, Sept. 30, 1988, p. 29.

8. "After the Ball, How America Will Conquer its Fear and Hatred of Gays in the 90's" by Marshall Kirk and Hunter Madsen, Doubleday, 1989, p. 179.

9. "Competing Ethical Systems" by James Hitchcock, *Imprimis*, April 1981, Copyright 1981, Hillsdale College.

10. "Love of Heavy Rock May be Tied to Teen Drugs, Sex" AMA Neuhaus News Service; *The Grand Rapids Press*, Sept. 22, 1989.

11. "Hate, Rape and Rap" by Tipper Gore. *The Washington Post*, 1/8/90.

Chapter 13

1. Richard A. Posner, *Law and Literature*, (Cambridge, MA: Harvard University Press, 1988), p. 311.

Chapter 14

1. See the excellent essay "The Almost-Chosen People: Why America is Different" by Paul Johnson published in 1985 by The Rockford Institute, 934 North Main Street, Rockford, Illinois 61103. And also Benjamin Hart, *Faith and Freedom: The Christian Roots of American Liberty* (Dallas; Lewis and Stanley, Publisher, 1989).

2. James J. Kilpatrick, "A Meditation for Independence Day," *National Review*, July 4, 1986, p. 26.

3. George Will, "Nonsense About Church & State," *The Washington Post*, July 9, 1989, p. B7.

4. Rena Pederson, "Whether Christianity in this Polyglot World?," *The Orange County Register*, January 22, 1990.

5. Paul C. Vitz, *Censorship: Evidence of Bias in Our Children's Textbooks* (Ann Arbor, Michigan: Servant Books), p. 65.

Chapter 15

1. "Some kids agree in survey: Rape ok if Date Costs Money" by Adelle Banks. *Los Angeles Herald Examiner*, Tuesday, May 8, 1988, A-14.

2. Malamuth, N.M., Heim, M. & Feshbach, S. (1980) *Journal of Personality and Social Psychology*, pp. 38, 399–408.

3. Reuters News Service, February 21,1990.

4. Randy Shilts, (*And the Band Played On*), New York: Penguin Books, 1987), pp. 21, 200.

INDEX